CULTIVATING JOY TO EXCEL
AT BUSINESS AND LIFE

NICO HUMAN PHD

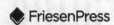

FriesenPress

One Printers Way
Altona, MB R0G 0B0
Canada

www.friesenpress.com

Copyright © 2021 Nico Human
First Edition — 2021

ISBN
978-1-03-911201-8 (Hardcover)
978-1-03-911200-1 (Paperback)
978-1-03-911202-5 (eBook)

Business & Economics, Leadership

Distributed to the trade by The Ingram Book Company

Table of Contents

"I have worked with Nico in a variety of one-on-one and team settings—here is the thing, Nico is one of those extraordinary humans that always emanates a positive energy. You can feel it and it flows into your world. In this book, Nico reminds us that we are special, unique, and deserve the very best life has to offer. Nico has taken his energy and zest for joy and translated it into a 'how-to' guide so everyone can have that special energy. Whatever you choose to adopt from the book—you will start to see your 'joy' bucket shine. Great read—great tips—great outcomes!"

Shelley McDade, President, Sunshine Coast Credit Union

"The community of people I work with and serve in our businesses are on a mission towards being a truly great workplace. The easy adjustments were material, i.e. compensation and equipment. The hard work has been culture shaping. We have chosen to become more vulnerable and words like love, pain, gratefulness, and joy are becoming part of our everyday language and experience. I commend Nico for spotlighting joy and engaging the business community in the joy conversation. This book read alone stands to shape how leaders lead. This story entered into by a group of people will truly aid transformation. Be a Joy Farmer. Enjoy!"

W. Scott Brown, President & CEO, Fifth Avenue Real Estate Marketing Ltd., Epic Real Estate Solutions. Executive Director, Baker West Real Estate Inc.

"I have had the pleasure of knowing and working alongside Nico for many years. Nico is a man I have come to respect and admire deeply, both in daily life and in business. The insights he shares in this book come from personal experiences, and his is a life well lived. I am honored to call him my friend."

Ken Falk, Owner and President, Twin Maple Group of Companies.

"Nico Human radiates 'joy' in all that he does, and this book captures the essence of the joy we all need in our lives. As a gifted leadership coach, his insights and practical instructions will guide you through how to live everyday life and make a difference in the life of others. Whether you are leading your family or a team in business, this book will show you how to cultivate and nurture joy to share it with others and live a life filled with purpose. You will be challenged, encouraged, and inspired to make changes in your life that will last for eternity."

Penny Fuchihara, Executive Director, Willingdon Church.

"The story of finding joy through the metaphor of farming is easy to follow, and like fruits and vegetables, is loaded with 'nutrients' to bring happiness to you, whether it be in your personal or professional life."

Luke O'Hare, Director, Logistics and Supply Chain Distribution, Urban Barn

"I had a unique opportunity to be part of a set of activities led by Nico. At work, as leaders, it brought us to a state of constant awareness, reducing stress and burnout at the same time that it helped develop trust among us. I can assure you that if you are looking for impactful changes in yourself in ways that you can benefit from it in your day-to-day, at work and in your life, you should look for Nico!"

Pedro Catoira, ScrumMaster, Bananatag

"Nico Human's observations on cultivating joy in our lives are eye-opening, thoughtful, and always uplifting. He reminds us that if we choose to open ourselves to it, joy is all around us. And the more attention we pay to it, the more we will find. I have had the privilege to know Nico as a business/life coach, Mackay CEO Forums Chair, and as a wise and caring friend. I know that readers of *Joy Farming* will harvest value from it.

Ron Sowden, CEO, DEKORA

"Nico is a calm, inspiring leader who has had a tremendous and positive impact on me since I met him one year ago. Joy Farming is an insightful look into Nico's past and present that can help anyone to a better, and more importantly, a joyful future."

Jason Fawcett, President, Kelson Group
Property Management

"Maya Angelou has an insightful quote that has been a guiding principle throughout much of my life, 'At the end of the day people won't remember what you said or did, they will remember how you made them feel.' A person who is able to make an employee, a colleague, a friend, an acquaintance or even a stranger feel valued, energized, and respected will be a person who has success in whatever they endeavour. Our management team spent an entire day with Nico who helped us to better understand the barriers that periodically impact our ability to work functionally as a group. The day was insightful, emotional, and challenging, but at the end of the day we knew each other a little better, understood the basis of many of our personal challenges, and were motivated to work on our own growth opportunities. Nico's philosophy of 'Working Above the Line' has been as impactful to our team as Maya Angelou's famous words have been to me. When we find ourselves veering from the path, it just takes a kind reminder from a co-worker to 'Work Above the Line' to quickly get us back on course."

Dan Painchaud, Operations General Manager, Scamp Transport Ltd.

"If you want to harvest the most and best from life and career, Joy Farming is a must-read. Nico brings his wisdom and experience to help readers face their biggest challenges to success."

Michael McKnight, President and CEO, United Way of the Lower Mainland.

"Nico is a leader that is full of energy, charisma, and wisdom. He exhibits the joy of life that he writes about. He has enriched my life with his advice and coaching of how to cultivate joy in life and inspires me to be a better leader. His book reads like he is right there with you, coaching you every step of the way with practical and insightful ways to find joy in all arenas in your life."

Jennifer Cho, CFO, Engineers and Geoscientists BC

"I've had the good fortune of Nico chairing my Mackay Forum group, and I can think of no better person to speak on joy. As one might practice yoga, meditation, an art, or a musical instrument, Nico is dedicated to his practice of farming joy. Nico is not only pursuing his passion, he's happy to share his learnings with others to inspire them to bring joy to their leadership. I am grateful for the time I spend with Nico. His joy is contagious!"

Cameron Grieve, Vice President, Investments,
LOTUS Capital

"I have known Nico personally and professionally for over twenty years. He brings limitless energy to any setting and has the ability to instantly and authentically connect with his audience. This book brings out his positive and joyful outlook to life and work even when addressing difficult topics—an absolute must-read."

Mimi Vanderwalt – Director, Sales Solutions, TELUS

"The endearing joy lessons Nico gleaned from his farming grandparents as a young boy, he continues to pass on to leadership teams today as an engaging leadership consultant. As you read this delightful work, you will be inspired to live more fully and find practical ways to farm for joy within the multiple spheres of everyday life."

Ray Harms-Wiebe, Lead Pastor, Willingdon Church

"Thought-provoking and enlightening. Nico has interwoven his incredible life story, farming background and life experiences into a powerful message of finding JOY in life."

Joe Falk, GM, Fraser Valley Specialty Poultry

*To Estelle, my wife, encourager extraordinaire,
love of my life.
To Sarie, my mom, for always believing in me,
who gave me life.
Love you both to eternity and beyond ...*

Introduction

> When I was five years old, my mother always
> told me that happiness was the key to life.
> When I went to school, they asked me what
> I wanted to be when I grew up. I wrote down
> *happy*. They told me I didn't understand
> the assignment, and I told them they didn't
> understand life.
>
> — John Lennon

Through my coaching practice and role as a MacKay
CEO Forums[1] chair, where we populate the world with
inspiring leaders, I am in a privileged position to watch and
learn from some amazing leaders. I observe them doing
great things and changing the world for the better. I also
witness their struggles and their realness as human beings

---

[1] You can visit the MacKay CEO Forums website here:
https://mackayceoforums.com

on their journey of leadership and life. I see how they face hardships.

I also see how they—like you and me—only want to be happy. When all is said and done, they want to be able to sit down and look back on a job well done and clients well-served, along with strong, positive relationships with their staff and families.

I've noticed that the leaders who have more joy are more effective, have more productive teams, attract better talent, and serve their clients better. Joyful leaders, in the words of John Lennon, *understand the assignment*. They're good at living life.

So, as a leader, my first quest is to—every day and in every way—be on the hunt for happiness and joy. I want to fill my tank to overflowing. I want to have so much joy that it spills over to all the people I touch. I want to be able to withstand the onslaughts of negativity and evil. I want to be able to focus my thoughts, reframe them, and live a positive life. I want to be a master of my emotions, and through tools like daily gratitude, find joy.

I realize that this is constant work. Some days will be easier. Some days will be extremely challenging! Like a farmer, I want to continuously work to plant, water, feed, nurture, and protect my joy crop. Like a farmer, I want to have faith in the Higher Hand who creates the soil and brings the rain. Like a farmer, I want to rejoice and share my crop with the world when it is ready.

We all want to be happy. It's a universal desire. Ask anyone what they want out of life, and almost all will say they want *happiness*. Ask parents what they want most for their children, and again it will be something like, "I just want them to be happy."

Happiness, however, is fleeting at best. We can be happy in the moment, but it's also relative, depending on our mental state.

If we decide to be happy, we can be happy. And there's the famous happiness equation: where your life condition is in comparison to your expectations. You are happy when your life condition is equal to your expectations. If your life condition falls short of your expectations—when you've got these high hopes, but reality doesn't come close to it—you feel unhappy; you are in a place of scarcity, a place of need, a place of want.

On the other hand, when you've received so much more than you ever expected, you may feel guilty that you've received all these extra blessings that you may not have necessarily worked for. Whereas, when you don't have enough, you may feel inferior, and that's not a good place to be in either.

Happiness, therefore, is related to your expectations and your life condition. It, however, is also a choice. It's been proven that some people can be happy despite anything that comes their way. They simply decide to be happy. It's a decision. What may make me unhappy, may make you happy. There's the old question: is the glass is half empty or half full?

How do you see the glass?

Some people, supposedly the optimists, see the glass as half full. Others, the pessimists, see the same glass as half empty. Then there are people who don't see the glass half full or half empty; they just see the beautiful glass. It's an altogether different mindset—much more creative. Recently I heard a story about a little one who was asked whether they saw the glass half full or half empty. The little one said, "But that glass is full. It's half full of water and half full of air, so it's *full*."

To me, happiness is this decision, this emotion, this fleeting feeling that can leave in a moment. But it's a building block of joy; it's a means to an end. Happiness is not the destination, but it's part of your journey. To me, joy is much deeper than just mere happiness. It is something that comes to you when all the other pieces have fallen into place. You can decide to be happy. Joy, on the other hand, finds you. In that moment of joy, you realize you've got it; you've received joy. It is something you receive from a bigger place, from outside of yourself.

Joy is an outcome—the product of a life lived in such a way that you are not only finding joy every day, but also able to share it with those who your life touches. Gratefulness is a big part of it. Being in control of your emotions and able to withstand the onslaughts of the world are crucial. There are many additional factors—such as a strong mind, mastering your time and finding your purpose—which we'll explore in this book.

Joy, to me, is also a gift. Joy comes to me often when I'm singing in a big choir, especially our church's mass choir. I'm a Christian. I enjoy the worship experience. When we practice the same song over and over, we gradually get better at it, and I'll possibly reach a state of happiness. But then we go on stage, singing in front of the congregation with our full symphony orchestra. By the second or the third church service—when we've sung the same songs at least three times in full voice—there's this moment where I just feel open and connected to Heaven. It's this joyful place, of music, the vibrations of the orchestra throughout my body, my state of mind, and the people around me—knowing we're all in this together—and I'm just filled with joy.

This same joyful experience can come to you when you are in awe of nature, when you're with your loved ones, or you hold a tiny baby for the first time. Joy sure found me when I first held my newborn kids!

Joy is also contagious. I've seen that leaders who are able to live and work in a place of joy are way more inspirational to their team. Everyone wants to follow someone who leads them to this joyful place where the journey is fun! This energy is infectious and attracts better behaviour. Relationships improve. Clients are served better. Some leaders actually develop waiting lists of top talent who want to work in their companies. In the end, it is no surprise that their companies become more resilient, more profitable, and more able to stand the test of time.

Throughout this book, we'll be exploring ways to set you up in a place where you'll be able to receive joy in your life and share it with those around you at work, at home, and everywhere. Anyone your life touches. You'll also learn how this joy will enrich your team, your business, your family, your life!

I'm no joy maker. I don't know how to manufacture joy. But I do know how to grow it like a farmer.

Farming means you're working with something precious; you're working with life, and you're there as the custodian of that life. You can plant the seed, you can prepare the soil, you can water it, you can weed it (if there are weeds), and you can prune it when it's time, but in the end, you're just farming with it. If it's a growing plant, that's your job as a farmer. You're not creating the life. You are simply there as a person, a conduit, a custodian to help this plant grow.

This is the role that I can play in bringing joy to you. I cannot make the joy. I cannot create it. My role is to present you with tools, tips, and techniques to prepare the way (like a farmer prepares the land) to help you practice planting and watering the symbolic joy seeds, until you become better and better at it. Going forward, you'll become a farmer—a farmer of joy.

Also, when you become a joy farmer and you're farming joy for yourself, you will naturally start spreading joy to others. It's impossible to be bursting with joy and keep it all to yourself! A gift to this world would be us all becoming joy farmers together, where joy farming is the ultimate goal. And as we work together and progress forward, one day, we'll just realize that we all are truly blessed. The joy has found us because we farmed it, and the fruit of joy is there, pretty much like a harvest. What a joyous day when the fruit is there!

I am quite a keen gardener. I've got potted plants all over my house. I especially love orchids. They bloom only once a year. Once orchids lose their blossoms, they become pretty ugly. It's just these leather-like leaves in a pot, but as a gardener—or a farmer, if you prefer—you know that you have to just keep taking care of them, giving them their nutrition and their water on time, to keep them going through the whole growing period. You can forget about the orchids, but weekly you have to take care of them. Then one day out of the blue, when you least expect it, out will come a shoot! And within a couple of days, there will be the first little blossom. Then the next shoot and the next blossom. That's the joy of farming—when you least expect it, it'll surprise you.

I've often been surprised through my coaching work by the ways in which high-performing leaders plant the seeds and nurture their joy crop.

The five most important ways they do this are:

1. They show incredible grit and determination when the occasion demands it.
2. They constantly work to master their emotions.
3. They relentlessly stick to their time-mastery system.
4. They constantly choose happiness. They make the decision to be happy. They also know that happiness is an essential building block in their quest to find joy.
5. They know their *sweet spot* and actively live their purpose.

My hope is that all my experiences, and the tips and tools they gave me, will help you find your own true joy.

My prayer is that you will soon be able to start overflowing with joy and sharing it with the world.

Together we will make this planet a better place for all of us!

Chapter 1: Prepare the Soil

Strengthen Your Mind to Create an Environment of Joy

My joy journey started on my paternal grandfather's farm. Here, away from the disapproving gaze of my critical dad, I found a place where I felt welcome and loved.

I was a precocious little boy, very active, and a bit too lively for some people's liking. My *Ouma* (Grandma), ruler of the homestead, would often kick me out of the house to go "play outside." I loved talking and discovering. I loved singing and performing the recitations I'd learnt at school. *Oupa* (Grandpa) was my audience during the day, my family at night.

There was no electricity on the farm. Burning candles and paraffin lamps was expensive, so our daily rhythm closely followed sunlight hours. The modern-day comforts we have today simply did not exist then; you needed grit and endurance to live through the cold of winter and the heat of summer. My grandparents did not seem to be bothered, but this city boy can still remember those nightly trips to the bathroom through the freezing cold house!

Life on the farm wasn't just about grit though. There was also the joy of the evening routine. After dinner, *Oupa* would wind up the cuckoo clock in the *voorhuis* (the front rooms, kept clean and neat for visits from minor community celebrities, like the *dominee*: the local pastor). The *voorhuis* was normally out of bounds for a young one like me, but I would sometimes be allowed to go with *Oupa*, and on a good day even be allowed to pull down the two chains to wind up the clock! Oh, what a happy day that would be.

We would then move to the *sonkamer* (the sunroom, equivalent to today's living room) where the family would assemble to wait for *Oupa* to do *boekevat* (evening Bible study). He would read from the big, hefty family Bible that contained our family tree. We had to listen because after reading, he would ask us young ones some questions to see whether we had paid attention! Then the real fun started. The kids were invited to entertain the adults. It was my small window of opportunity to perform for a captive audience before everyone headed off to bed. I was always the most enthusiastic!

My first entrepreneurial initiative took place on one of these nights. I had learnt a hymn called *Heugelike Tyding* (*Joyful Tiding*) but could not properly pronounce the word *heugelike*. My uncle loved it when I sang this song; it brought a smile to his face every time. So earlier in the day, he had offered me a *tickey* (a coin worth two-and-a-half cents back then) to sing *Heugelike Tyding* for him that evening after *boekevat*. So there we were. He turned to me, took out the coin, and with a flourish, he put it on the table and asked me to sing. I took the coin, put it in my pocket, smiled sweetly, and then turned to each one of the other adults, asking for their *tickeys*! They were going to be in the audience, so they had to pay admission as well, right?

A *tickey* back then could buy you an ice cream bar. I had a joyous time the next time we went to town, as I had enough *tickeys* to buy everyone an ice cream!

From *Oupa*, I learnt that you are responsible for your own happiness; it takes some sacrifice and grit. He would be up very early (before the rooster crowed) to do his morning rounds. I was always invited along, but he would only call on me once. I learnt very quickly that if I jumped out of bed immediately, I would make it in time to leave the house with him. If I dawdled, if my warm bed enticed me to linger, he would be gone without looking back. During the winter months, it was hard! Since the house was not heated, the *donskombers* (down quilt) created a cozy nest overnight, but I would have to leave comfort behind if I wanted to experience the joy of being with *Oupa*. So I had to learn to not think and just do it. It took grit to get out of bed, especially for a small boy!

This kind of grit is needed from you and me, even today, if we want to reach a place of joy. It's the sacrifices we need to make, the comforts and luxuries we need to forego, in order to do the work that will ultimately result in our long-term joy. But how can you learn to have more grit?

When coaching leaders and their teams, I've found that following this four-step approach works quite well:

1. Train your brain

2. Control your breathing

3. Focus your thoughts

4. Spend most of your time in a positive state or *above the line*, as we call it

Use Grit to Train Your Brain for Joy

The mind is incredibly powerful. Leaders are aware of their thought processes, especially how devastating and disempowering it can be if they allow their thoughts to run wild. They know how to buckle down, still their minds, and focus on what's important.

It takes grit to harness the power of the brain. It is so easy to become distracted and unfocused, especially today with the constant overstimulation of our senses and brains by the media. The trap is always there to just reach for the next thing that clamours for our attention. Instead, throughout my career, what I observed was that these leaders practiced mental toughness to stay focused on the essential and to lead their team through the chaos.

Use Your Brain's Three Parts Properly to Bring More Joy to Your Life: A traffic light can serve us well as a metaphor for the brain's three parts, which we are going to discuss here.

The brain's energy is very similar to the traffic light's colours and what they symbolize.

One part of the brain—let's call it the red brain or red energy—represents the central portion of the brain, called the *reptilian brain* or *amygdala*. Our instincts live here. This is the part of the brain that receives blood, and therefore oxygen, first. It has been crucial for our survival as a species, keeping our ancestors safe by triggering one of three responses: fight (when he was cornered by a lion and had to fight for his life), freeze (when a poisonous snake had not seen her and was slithering by), or flight (when they were pursued by a rival tribe out to kill them both).

Today, unfortunately, this red brain is what causes most of our stress. It still keeps us safe, but when was the last time you encountered a poisonous snake slithering by? Today's triggers that garner these types of responses are often a myriad of stimuli that come with modern life. The ping of a text arriving can send us into a state of high alert. That nasty email from a disgruntled boss can stop us in our tracks. Sometimes the constant barrage of sounds and lights from our busy lives sends us fleeing to a place of quiet and calm.

The lesson here is how to harness the benefits of the red brain and not get drawn into ancient responses. What we need to understand here, and learn to expect, is that this part of the brain gets blood first. That is how our anatomy works.

Next, let's look at what we can call the yellow part of the brain, also called the *emotional brain* or the *limbic system*. This is where our emotions live. This part serves to make us aware of what is going on around us. Our emotions are like the gauges on the dashboard of a car or airplane. Similar to how gauges give us a reading of what is going on in the engine or body of the plane, our emotions give us a reading of what is going on in our surroundings. Negative emotions normally warn us, helping us to stay safe. Positive emotions help be better and enjoy a higher quality of life.

What's important to remember is that your emotions come after the fight, freeze, or flight response. It's the next step, and it tells us more about what is going on for us and around us.

The third part, the green brain, or the *intellectual brain*, lives in the front part of the brain just behind our foreheads in the prefrontal cortex or neocortex. Humans have well-developed green brains. Reasoning lives here. It also allows us to have higher thought processes. Curiosity, creativity, that type of thing, is at our disposal when we fire up this part of our brain. We can reason. We can plan. We can create. We can become curious of how things work—and make things better. We can ask why and find a better path!

It is a bit ironic that, when I was asked to start training teams of leaders, I chose the symbol of the traffic light to illustrate the inner workings of our brains. It reminded me of *Oupa* and his trepidation with modern developments (for his time) like traffic lights.

On the farm, *Oupa* was in his element. But the necessary weekly trip into town to buy provisions and deliver products would take him out of his comfort zone. In town, he was known and loved by all. He was called *Oom Nic* (Uncle

Nic). His full name was Nicolaas; I was named after him. I would accompany him on his rounds to the bank, the pharmacy, the bakery, and other shops, with our first and last stop always being the co-operative to drop off products on the way in and pick up supplies on the way out.

On the way back, when we stopped at the first farm gate, *Oupa* would always, with a sigh of relief, comment that it was great to be back on the farm.

The farm was his domain. It was in his blood. And yet, although the town was not his real stomping ground, he could *make the town work*. Perhaps it was because there were no robots in town.

Oupa, with a passion, hated the city's robots! This is what we called traffic lights, in both my first language, Afrikaans, and also in English, the official business language of South Africa. How they got called robots is a mystery. This was one of the idiosyncrasies of the country. Popular belief is that they were—when first introduced to replace traffic policemen—called robot lights or robot policemen, which then got truncated with time.

Oupa would plan his route to our house so that he would miss every robot along the way! He must have driven straight to our house every time! I have no memory of him driving in the city. He would take the easiest way to our house, park the car, and only drive it straight out to the city again when they departed.

Oxygen in Your Lungs
– Joy Fuel for Your Brain

In order to grow, crops need carbon dioxide during the day and oxygen during the night. It is their fuel. Human beings need oxygen too, but we need something more. We need joy, and that joy also needs oxygen.

It is important to note an interesting biological fact about the human body: it takes on average six seconds for the blood to flow to your intellectual brain. Remember blood always goes to the reptilian brain first. Our bodies are designed to keep us safe, first and foremost. When our red brains are triggered, like whenever *Oupa* saw a traffic light, blood flow stops to other parts of the brain and organs not needed for survival.

For example, there is no time for intellectual thought when you have a split second to react, or else you'll be eaten alive! Your legs will need all the help they can get to get you going as fast as you can! This is where the blood flow is directed to, bringing oxygen to those leg muscles working overtime!

Something similar happens when we are in a highly emotional state. When our emotions—especially the negative ones—get really loud, we start acting out of a place of fear, or anger, or whatever emotion is running us at that time. The point is, in our emotional brain, our emotions are running us—we are not in control of them. This is a place far removed from joy. A place where we can get stuck if we are not able to show the grit needed to make better choices.

We need to think of what we are supposed to do when approaching a set of traffic lights and then apply that to how we control our brains.

For us to shift out of the instinctive or emotional mode, to be able to control our panicked thoughts and get into a state of calm green brain energy, we need to get oxygen to our prefrontal cortexes. We need to play for time to allow the blood to reach that front part of our brains! Research has shown that at least six seconds are needed.

What follows is an exercise I teach my clients. My recommendation to you, the reader, is throughout this book, if you enjoy what you are reading, make a note and come back to these exercises later. If, however, you want to try out the exercises right away, you can do so as you go along.

Now, continuing with the traffic light symbol, I use the acronym STOP to describe the process of shifting from an instinctive mode to a calm place of reasoning in your intellectual brain.

When you feel those impulses to fight, freeze, or flee, or if you become aware of those negative emotional states, like feelings of fear or anger, this is what you need to do:

1. **S**top your thoughts and whatever you are doing in that moment.

   Like at a red traffic light, you need to stop to stay safe and make sure that the people around you are safe as well. There is no negotiation; there is no hesitation. You simply need to stop immediately.

You are not allowed to say another word or send off an email or do anything that will, in any case, come back to bite you.

2. **T**ake a breath.

If there is enough time, take a slow deep breath for over four seconds. Hold it for four seconds. Breathe out for four seconds. Hold it for four seconds.

Repeat this process for three or four cycles. This is called Square Breathing—think of a square and work with your breath, as you move around the square, four seconds per side.

You may not always have the time to do Square Breathing. Instead take one deep breath and hold it before slowly releasing the air. The trick here, whether you do the full Square Breathing or just a single sustained breath, is to focus on your exhales, as the slowness of it is a signal to your brain to calm down.

3. **O**bserve. Are you feeling better? Are you calm? If not, you have to do some more breathing until this is the case.

4. **P**roceed with what you were doing before.

If you were involved in a conversation, you are now able to access your creativity, your discernment, and all the wonderful gifts your intellectual brain brings you. You can be curious because you have risen above your instincts and emotions. In this state, you are able to do infinitely better!

If it was an email that you were about to send off, have a reread. In the email draft, find the anger (if you were angry before you started your breathing exercise). Find the self-doubt. Find the defensiveness. Best yet, rewrite the email using the green brain power of your intellectual brain. I can assure you it will be much better and save you heartache and lots of time in the long run!

The full STOP exercise is described in more detail in my article[2], which can be found on my website.

When the best version of you shows up, when you are functioning out of your intellectual brain, you will not only find joy, you will also start spreading it!

In business, your instincts show up a little differently. When we feel totally overwhelmed, we may want to quit. Quit the task. Quit the job. Quit life. We want to run away from our problems. This is pretty much the same as our ancestors fleeing from danger. Flight.

When we feel stuck, when we stop moving forward, we may retreat into ourselves. We may put up an impenetrable wall and become unreachable to those around us, pretty much trying to become unseen. We are frozen.

Then there are hot-blooded people like me. Whenever we are challenged, whenever we feel threatened, our fuses get shorter and shorter. We work harder. We attack

---

[2] https://joyfarming.ca/square-breathing/

the problem. Sometimes we even attack the person! We fight. This still is my basic instinct today, but I have learnt over the years not to act on this instinct. I am aware that this is my natural tendency, and I have learnt to simply become curious about this feeling and recognize it when it raises its ugly head. The coping strategies I have mastered allow me to better coach those who share similar instincts. It has made me stronger and a better coach.

How do your instincts show up?

Whatever the case may be, the proven formula to get us out of trouble is to stop, breathe, get curious about what our emotions are telling us, and then use our intellectual brain power to move us forward.

Every Second Counts when Getting to a Place of Joy

To shift out of the instinctual or emotional mode, the general rule is to slow down for that crucial six seconds, breathe deeply, and allow the blood to reach our intellectual brains. This works 99% of the time.

If you tend to procrastinate, it is actually better not to give your intellectual brain any chance to consider it whatsoever! Whenever you feel that pang of guilt when you're about to procrastinate on a task, you need to act immediately, definitely within five seconds. If you give your intellectual brain any chance of getting involved, you are going to reason with yourself and will find a reason why you can do the task later, or try and give it to someone else, or perhaps not even do it at all!

What you need to do is to immediately take the first small step to start the task. Let the fear, the guilt, the excitement, or whatever feeling is with you in that moment, drive your next action. If you think of the whole task, how big it is, it may overwhelm you and cause you to stop.

Focusing on a simple first step is easier for the brain to process. It may be as small as clearing your desk and getting a fresh sheet of paper and pen ready. It may be opening up your email and typing in the subject line for the first email. Anything small will get you started. If you then stay in that space and simply add the next step, and the next steps after that one, soon you will find yourself engrossed in the task. Oh, joyful place! You've beaten the Procrastination Devil!

This technique became a game changer for a young leader I recently coached. She was stuck and felt over-whelmed. She was just not getting the important tasks done on her daily to-do list—tasks that would move the needle for her and for the company. She was super dili-gent and got tons of things done every day, but some of the more complex, important tasks kept slipping down and often off her list. Her team was starting to notice. Her reputation started to suffer. It was not good.

When she described her daily process of working through her to-do list, I realized that she was overthinking her tasks, especially the more complex ones. Because it was easier to get the simple tasks done, she would do those first to feel the joy of completing those tasks. The important, more complex tasks got her into trouble, because she would start finding reasons why she should not do the task right in that moment. When her rational brain kicked in—that green energy of creativity—her brain would help her find reasons to delay the task, such as: *It's too complex. I need help from someone else. It would be best to do the task when I'm fresh in the morning.* The list went on and on. Her brain was actually working against her and sabotaging her productivity!

My coaching focused on helping her discover the precise emotion triggered when she landed on one of these tasks. She described the feeling as being stopped by a roadblock; something that was in her way and stopping her progress. She felt it was like an irritation, a bother—a mild, but unmistakable feeling. She even made a bit of a grimace when she described it! I asked her to lock in on that feeling, so that she would be able to recognize it whenever it reared its ugly head.

With the emotion identified, we worked on a plan of action for her to follow whenever she felt that feeling. A plan she had to embark on *immediately* when she felt that feeling. Once the feeling arrived, within the next few seconds, she had to simply identify the first step of working on that complex task and do it right away. That step then led to the next step and the next step and so forth, until the task was completed.

It changed the way she handled her daily tasks. Her Procrastination Devil was tamed! Within a week, she made major inroads on her backlog. Her productivity improved, her reputation was repaired, and soon she was finding joy at the end of a productive day again!

Focus Your Thoughts on Joy

The homestead was *Ouma's* domain. Here she reigned. *Oupa* may have been the boss on the farm itself, but this was where *Ouma* took the lead. She was very stern and conscientious, but we all knew that she had a wicked sense of humour just below the surface. All you needed to do, when she caught you in some mischief, was get her to crack up laughing, and you could get away with the proverbial murder. Well, we grandkids could. I'm not so sure her own kids could get away with it that easily.

Today, looking back on it, I realize that the homestead and its surroundings were a veritable small business cluster all on its own. There were the extensive poultry runs and coops. *Ouma* headed up the production of both eggs and poultry meat. I recall tons of chickens, turkeys, ducks, geese, and even Muscovy ducks. All were running freely during the day and had to be put into their coops at night, safe from the attack of jackals and other night creatures.

Just beyond the poultry runs were the pigsties. It was quite the spectacle to watch these ungainly creatures at feeding time. They would eat anything! Household waste, sour milk from the dairy operation, rotten vegetables, and much more. They slopped everything down in big gulps, accompanied by the sounds of grunting and squealing. Whenever we kids showed less-than-impeccable manners at the dinner table, *Ouma* would tell us we ate like pigs, stopping us in our tracks!

The vegetable gardens were next to the house. They were quite large. Irrigation came from the dam next to the garden.

This was an above-ground, circular structure filled with cool, underground water with some water lilies floating on the surface. Next to the dam was the *windpomp* (windmill)—a tall steel structure with a mini Eiffel tower-like appearance and one huge circular multi-bladed rotor on top. It always creaked when its flat tail vane found a change in the wind's direction. I can still remember the *thump-thump* sound it made when it started to pump water from great depths. And oh, the joyful sound when that water started flowing into the dam!

The orchards were beyond. This was my favourite place to go to when I wanted to be alone. Over a bit of a rise, the orchards were just out of sight, away from the main activities at the house. Lower down, it was cooler, and here is where I was surrounded by fruit trees: peaches, the occasional pear tree, and then the apples. My favourite was the apples. I can still recall the sights, and more importantly the smells, of the apples. I would close my eyes, so I could focus on the joy of smelling the blossoms in springtime or the apples themselves when they were hanging on the trees.

This was also *Ouma*'s favourite place to escape to. With the busyness of the homestead a good distance away, this was the place where she could catch her breath. The sights, and especially the smells, gave her a welcome respite from her daily responsibilities. A welcome break in a busy day. She delighted in it.

May I invite you to join me for a trip to the orchard? I'd love for you to also experience those sights and smells.

We can travel to the orchard with a simple exercise I use in my training workshops to show people how powerful the mind can be and also how easy it is to focus your mind. Grit doesn't have to be hard; it can just be discipline. The discipline to focus.

I call my exercise, *The Apple*.

This is how it goes. I use these very words:

> *Please find a comfortable way to sit. Uncross your arms and legs. Let them rest lightly, but solidly. Feel your body grounded in one place. Breathe easily and focus your thoughts on feeling every sensation in your body. Follow your breath as it comes in, lingers, and then leaves your lungs.*

> *I am inviting you to come on a short journey with me. If you feel comfortable enough, I invite you to close your eyes.*

> *Picture yourself walking outside in nature. It's a beautiful sunny day, and you can feel the sun's warmth on your arms and face. As you walk, you see a tree in the distance. When you approach it, you can see some ripe apples hanging from its branches.*

> *You reach up and pick an apple. You see a fresh drop of dew glistening off its skin, catching a ray of sunlight. You turn the apple in your hands, bring it to your nose, and smell it. As you take a bite, its flavours fill your mouth. You slowly chew and feel*

it in the back of your mouth before swallowing its
flesh. You savour it for a moment, and all the cares
of the world are left behind.

When you are ready, please open your eyes and
come back to the room.

Once everyone brings their focus back to the room, I ask about their experiences. I ask what colour their apples are. Most typically saw red apples. Some would say green. Some got specific and mentioned names, like Gala or Golden Delicious or Granny Smith. I also ask them what their apples taste like. I typically got "sweet," "cool," "tart." Some would remember it tasting crisp or cool on the tongue. Someone in the crowd would get carried away and tell us all about their whole journey discovering the apple orchard!

It's a fun exercise, and everyone is smiling at this point.

Then I ask the million dollar question:

Who, while thinking of their apple, had one single
thought about their troubles of the day? Who
spent one second thinking of their priorities and
tasks that are waiting, their worries or woes, or
any of the thousands of thoughts we normally
have in our minds all the time?

The answer always is: no one. If you are focused on your apple, it is quite easy to keep your mind in one place. If you involve your senses (like the feel of sunshine on your arms, or the smell and taste of the apple in our example), it makes it even easier. So with this exercise, you have trained your brain to focus.

This is a very important aspect to remember as far as your mental toughness or grit is concerned. This exercise clearly shows that you are able to control your mind by focusing your thoughts. Everyone can do this.

This skill becomes crucial when your mind is in a place that does not serve your best interest. An example of this is when we feel overwhelmed. Many people describe this as having thousands of thoughts. Thoughts that are not necessarily helpful or connected to one another that keep our minds captive, leaving us with feelings of anxiety and of being stuck.

This state is also called *ruminating*. When we get stuck in these ruminations, this is the time when our ability to focus our thoughts becomes very important. Unlike some farm animals, cattle, sheep, and goats are actually classified as ruminants, where rumination is a necessary process. For us, it is actually unproductive. We do not have stomachs with four parts where chewing the cud and ruminating is necessary for the digestion of our food. We ruminate on thoughts. It causes our brains to get stuck. It is not a good thing. We need to get unstuck. We need to move on.

Focusing your thoughts and then reframing them will allow you to turn your negative thought pattern into a productive one. You will be able to start thinking of solutions and possibilities, instead of being stuck in a spiralling pattern of despair. By just mastering this simple skill of focusing your thoughts, you will be able to start finding more happiness and joy in your life!

I use an apple for this exercise. You may want to use any other image, like a pear or a peach, accompanied by its sounds, tastes, smells, and feelings. Some people visualize their *happy place*, like a waterfall or a mountaintop. Others go back to a favourite time from their past when they felt safe and loved. It's up to you.

I'm an apple guy. So if you can—at any given moment during the day—replace your thoughts with the singular thought of a gorgeous apple, you will be able to escape any negativity and ultimately reach a place of joy. The point is that you will be able to control your thoughts. You will be able to steer your thoughts into a direction that will lead you to joy.

Stay Above The *Joy Line* for Joy-filled Days

Once my clients are able to successfully focus their thoughts, we start working on the second skill needed for mental mastery, called *The Line*. A well-known concept in the coaching world, *The Line* is a wonderful tool to help us navigate the negativity of our day and always strive to be in a positive frame of mind—especially when making key decisions.

We use this concept at MacKay CEO Forums all the time. I first learnt about it when I was a MacKay member many moons ago. Today I chair several MacKay CEO Forums, and we still use it all the time. I adapted what I learnt, and the GritGraphic© (see following page) was the result.

GritGraphic©

Your handy tool to live above the line and find joy.

Past
- Celebrate progress made
- Learn from mistakes
- Relive positive moments

Present
HAPPINESS ZONE
- In the moment
- Focused on positive thoughts
- Zapped and zapping

Future
- Visualize success
- Focus on what you want
- Focus on vision for the future

THE JOY LINE

- Worry and guilt
- Regret
- Relive mistakes

- Thousands of thoughts
- Stuck in the negative
- Sapped and sapping

- Visualize failure
- Focus on what you don't want
- Worry and anxiety
- Fear

joyfarming.ca

The *Joy Line* runs between thoughts that are negative (described as below the line) and thoughts that are positive (above the line). It looks at our present condition, as well as our thoughts about the past and future. If you dip below the line, you are going into negative territory and run the risk of being infected by the negativity virus. If you are above the line, you are in a positive frame of mind, able to make decisions, and live your life from that perspective.

This becomes a joy game changer for people with grit. They constantly work towards keeping their thoughts above the line.

This imaginary line is a great little tool to help you organize and control your thoughts and bring them to a place where your brain can be stimulated to function intellectually in the areas of possibility and creativity, instead of being stuck instinctively in the areas of fight, freeze or, flight. You start living positive days, you are happy in the moment, and it opens the door for joy to follow.

However, it is natural and normal for us to be constantly pulled below the line. We are surrounded by negativity every day. It weighs us down. Sometimes we do not have the energy to reframe our thoughts and lift ourselves above the line. Sometimes we may feel the need to be in that negative space for a while. This is very dangerous, as we may get trapped there. Negativity will lead us into a downward spiral. We call it the negativity virus at the MacKay CEO Forums.

We must allow each other to only spend a maximum of three minutes in that negative state to process our thoughts and feelings. Then it is time to find the energy to lift ourselves above the line, before irreparable damage is caused.

On the farm, *Oupa* was constantly watching his crops and animals for diseases. He knew that diseases would be lurking below the surface, hidden, and he had to look for telltale signs. During multiple days of rain, he would constantly be on the lookout for signs of root rot in the corn. He knew that, if left untreated, it could wipe out the entire harvest. Because it affected the roots, out of sight under the soil, he had to constantly watch the plant above ground for signs of the disease.

This is very similar to the image of negative thoughts below *The Joy Line* on the GritGraphic©. Whenever we find our thoughts heading into negativity land, or start noticing these behaviours in someone else, we need to act, and act fast.

This tool is very handy to constantly remind us to focus our thoughts to be in a place where it will help us become better. Here is how you can use the GritGraphic©:

1. **When thinking of the past**, whenever we are below the line and our thoughts are heading to a place of worry, guilt, or regret, or whenever we get stuck simply reliving past mistakes, we need to focus our minds and reframe our thoughts. Instead we can think of that mistake we made but in a different way. Instead of being trapped in the feeling of failure, we can reframe and think of what lessons we learnt.

We can use our intellectual brain to become curious about ensuring how we will not make that mistake again. Instead of reliving mistakes, we can shift our thoughts to relive positive moments, and we can celebrate the progress that was made.

In the past, it has happened to me where something that I, at the time, thought was a total disaster, later on became a pivotal moment in my journey of life. What seemed totally negative at the time turned out to be a blessing in disguise.

Something that I want to make very clear is that, by using this tool, we are refocusing the same experience in a positive light in order to move forward. It does not mean that the actual experience was something fully positive. We are not looking at life through rose-tinted glasses! We are merely learning from the experience and moving on to a place of possibility and creativity and growth, instead of being stuck in a place of negativity. The overall experience will still be in our memory banks as a mistake, a negative experience, but now it's an experience that we have learnt from and, most importantly, moved on from.

2. **When thinking in the present**, when we are instinctively below the line, we get bombarded by thousands of thoughts. It saps all our energy. We feel stuck and defeated. Because we have so many thoughts, we flit from one to the other. We are left exhausted and oftentimes in a state of anxiety. Stressful times! By simply focusing and then

reframing, we start living in the present. We focus on the positive thoughts. We get curious about how we can move forward, and soon we will feel our energy levels improving. In the next chapter, we will discuss how to master your emotions—this all comes into play when we live in the moment, maximizing our energy above the line.

We can only find true joy and happiness when living in the moment. By experiencing the here and now, we fully embrace life. How we feel, and how we choose to interpret the very moment we live in, determines our moment, our hour, our day, and eventually our whole life. We can look back on the past with happy memories, but that is all they are: memories. We can look to the future with expectations, but that is all they are: expectations. We live in the here and now. This is where our happiness and joy are determined.

3. **When thinking of the future**, below the line we visualize failure—what we don't want. We are ridden with worry, fear, and anxiety. When we focus on what we don't want, and we make plans with that in our minds, is it any surprise that we end up in exactly the place where we do not want to be? Instead, we should reframe our thoughts and focus on what we do want. What success will look like. If we visualize success, our positive thoughts will pull us in that direction. When we focus on a vision for the future, we are best equipped to move into that direction and make it reality.

Once my clients have this knowledge and have started the work to develop that muscle of constantly moving their thoughts above the line, they are well on their way to becoming mentally resilient; they have acquired grit.

When I was running a sizable transportation company (of about 100 employees) in British Columbia, we faced considerable challenges when Alberta's oil industry collapsed. This forced all the transportation companies from Alberta, our neighbour, to send their trucks into our service area, desperate to find work. They would undercut our rates and steal our customers, just to keep their trucks rolling! My team had to defend our turf. We had to be super positive and bring excellent service to our customers, even though the onslaught, at times, was quite overwhelming. My job was to keep the team positive and attack the problem with determination.

So I introduced them to the GritGraphic©.

I pasted the GritGraphic© in noticeable places around our offices. Nicely framed versions were hung in my office, in our reception area, and in our boardroom. Simple copies were posted on notice boards in all departments. I also made it available in an electronic version to everyone and anyone. (You can download yours from my Resources page[3].)

The GritGraphic© became a constant positive reminder for all of us, as I emphasized that it had to be used as a tool for encouragement and never judgement. It helped us all

[3] https://joyfarming.ca/wp-content/uploads/2021/06/Mental-Toughness-Chart.pdf

be better together, and we were able to maintain a positive mindset throughout this difficult time for the company.We were able to spread this energy to the rest of the company and to our customers. It served us well and enabled us to face this difficult time together. We were able to keep our key clients, allowing us to ride out the storm.

And as a team, our performance improved. We were there for each other and committed to each other's success. The silver lining of this difficult time was that the tool helped us stay positive, attack the problem, and slowly regain the company's profitability.

We need constant reminders to start living above the line. This system encompasses a whole series of new habits. But it's not easy to implement a new habit. It takes time, effort, and a will to be better. Once it becomes part of you, the way you show up and operate, it starts blessing you with the gifts of optimism, hope, and other positive emotions. And you will find yourself with renewed energy, increasing the joy in your life.

Once you introduce this positive system to your loved ones and colleagues, your joy tank will start filling up even more.

Once *The Line* and its system were introduced, we—as a leadership team—developed a simple gesture to encourage one another to constantly strive to keep our thoughts and words above the line. Whenever in conversation, anyone who became aware that you were drifting below the line, would make this simple gesture using both hands with palms upwards (forming the line), followed by a slow motion of pushing the palms upwards. This would encourage everyone to bring our conversation to a place where we could be able to use our intellects instead of our instincts to serve us better.

Successful leaders use grit to grow their happiness. Like a farmer growing a crop. They know that sustained happiness will bring them joy in the long run. But they know, to get there, they need to keep their thoughts above the line.

Where Happiness Lives: If you look at the GritGraphic©, you can pinpoint the area where happiness is found. Happiness is definitely above the line. When you fondly remember your favourite memories, the feeling you get is in the present. You feel it in the here and now. Also, you can, with anticipation, look forward to something promising or exciting waiting for you in the future, but again, the feeling you get—that feeling of giddy anticipation—you feel it in the here and now. Happiness lives above the line, in the here and now of the present.

I, therefore, encourage people to start living their lives, focusing on where they are in the moment. How do you feel? What is your body telling you? What does it need? What is your current emotion telling you? If we can focus on being present, to live our lives fully in the moment, we'll be happy and joy is bound to follow!

Did you know that happiness, in the end, comes down to you and only you? You get to make this decision, and yes, happiness is a decision. You are either happy or unhappy *with* your circumstances, or you can decide to be happy *despite* your circumstances.

On the farm, we did not have many luxuries—compared to today's circumstances, we lived in hardship; even back then it was worse than in the city—but we were happy. We went to bed with the chickens because the nights were dark, and it was too expensive to burn energy for heat and light. When you had to go to the bathroom in the middle of the night, you had to endure the cold, unheated house and get back to bed as quickly as possible! When I rose with *Oupa* very early, the cold and the hardship associated with it was simply part of the deal. We were happy *despite* these circumstances.

Living in the moment, in the here and now, is the only place where you can find happiness. This is where you get to make the decision whether you are happy or not. A simple happiness equation, a formula if you prefer, can be used to determine your happiness: **LC = E**, where **LC** is your circumstance or **L**ife Condition and **E** is your **E**xpectation. If your circumstances and your expectations align, you're happy. Things are going well. It feels like there's a balance. If your life conditions, however, are worse or lower than what you were expecting them to be—your expectations were either too high, or your life conditions ended up too low—you're not happy. You don't have a balance; you are in a place of want, scarcity. You want more. You may think that the opposite—when your life conditions turn out better than what you were expecting—would make you happy. But it normally does not last.

Then one of two things happens. You may set your bar so low that you realize you are actually cheating yourself. This is not the best you can do. It is not happiness. You are not really happy, and joy will not follow. Most people think the opposite, when reality turns out better than what you were expecting, is true happiness. And it does feel great for a while. The catch here is that this flings the door wide open for feelings of pride and superiority to start appearing. When we are in this state, we are not truly happy. Then, for most people anyway, doubts come up: *Why am I receiving all this? I don't deserve this. I have not worked for this*. Feelings of guilt replace any possible remaining strands of any happiness we may still have! A miserable place to end up at, really.

So, the bottom line is to reach a place where we constantly balance our expectation—which should not be too high or too low—with our life condition. That is where happiness lives.

If we find ourselves aiming for high expectations and constantly not reaching them, leaving us in a state of unhappiness, we need to ask ourselves whether the expectations were unrealistic. We need to make an adjustment. If we consciously want to stretch ourselves and the expectation is more like a goal, we need to take that into consideration. It is okay not to fully reach a goal—especially a stretch goal—if that was what you expected. It is our expectation that is at play here, not whether we reached the goal.

To address the flip side of the proverbial coin is important here too. If we find ourselves having really low, even mediocre, expectations, and we reach them quite easily, we also need to make an adjustment. Try setting your expectations a bit higher. Be a bit more ambitious. Playing it safe all the time will not bring us happiness. In the long run, we will feel left behind, even cheated. It will feel too much like failure.

With balance, we are able to arrive at the place where we can make the decision to be happy in a situation. When we add the additional ingredients, which this book is all about, we will start enjoying a joyful life.

I can still recall those moments early in the morning when *Oupa* and I were walking down the path to the milking operation. It was bitterly cold, but I was happy. I was happy to be with my hero, to enjoy his attention. My cup ran over with joy when he would put his big hand on my small head as we walked down the path. It was a feeling of belonging, of being accepted, of being safe. It was pure joy.

Helping Someone Get Above the Line Will Bring You More Joy: During a recent virtual coaching session with a client group, the question came up about how we can help someone who is having trouble staying positive. Someone who ends up dragging down those around them. Someone who kills the mood and destroys the productivity.

I first discussed with the client group how this person's behaviour was detrimental to the team's performance and how it was robbing them all of joy. Tolerating this type of behaviour is not only harmful in the short run, but over time it can be devastating to the team. Negativity is like a virus. It can spread like wildfire. One Negative Nelly can kill all the ideas, all the potential growth of a team, by shooting down all ideas. That behaviour will then spread to others, and soon it becomes the way the team operates, ingrained in the team culture. And it will keep spreading, if left unchecked. The team will become miserable.

I also introduced to them the real joy bringer in this situation—if you are able to help lift someone from this place of miserable negativity, it will make you feel great. You will feel as if you have made a contribution to make things better. Not only will you see how much better the other person is doing—and you were instrumental in helping the person get there—you will also see how it benefits the team. You will become a joy farmer yourself. A place of pure joy!

But how can you help someone get above the line?

A wise leader once gave me the simple formula: **MVE**.

MVE is a simple three-step process for you to help anyone who is in a negative frame of mind. The person may be sad. Or fearful. Or just simply negative and below the line.

The first step is to restrain yourself. Do not jump in with *helpful* suggestions! We, especially men, can very easily find ourselves going into fix mode. Don't do it! It's a trap!

Instead simply listen and then **Mirror** what you see and hear.

Phrases like, "I can see you are hurting," or "I hear your pain," can be very helpful. This language is very important, as it builds a connection between you and the other person. They feel heard. When you simply state what you see (like a mirror), there is no room for judgement. The person is left feeling that you are on their side; you are there to help them do what's best for them.

The next step is to **Validate** what is going on. Comments like, "It makes sense to me that you feel this way," or "I understand that you feel this way," will help. This allows the other person to relax and trust you and the process. They feel like they're in safe hands. They can open up and be vulnerable.

And then the most important step, show **Empathy**.

Simply be with the person. Support them. Be there for them. Empathy means you are alongside them, with you both simply looking at the problem. You are there for them, supporting them throughout the process. You are not there to fix them or the situation. You are simply there to support them throughout the process until, or if, they can come to their own solution.

Showing empathy should not be confused with showing sympathy. The latter action will lead to a much different, and in this case undesirable, outcome.

Empathy is when you come alongside the person, simply acknowledge what is going on, and assure them that you are there for them through thick and thin. You are vulnerable and feel close to them. You share the load. Sympathy, on the other hand, is when you come from a place of looking down on the other person. Since you are in a position of strength, it may look to them as if you are unaffected. What you may think are helpful suggestions for improvement may look to them as though you are judging the situation or the circumstances surrounding it. Brené Brown has a very helpful online video[4] that beautifully illustrates the difference between empathy and sympathy in a nutshell. It is well worth the watch.

The misconception is to show sympathy. Don't do it! Do not bring your own feelings into the picture. Avoid judgement! Sometimes we feel that if we start judging the other person in the problem or the situation itself, then the person we are trying to help will be well-served. That is not the case. It will leave the person stuck and will keep spreading the negativity. Don't do it!

[4] https://www.youtube.com/watch?v=HznVuCVQd10

Instead stay with empathy.

Simply stay focused on the person, understanding and acknowledging the feelings being expressed. Be patient. Listen. With the space and grace created, the person will have the best chance to move to above the line.

Let's all support our friends and colleagues when they most need us!

Only three steps: **M**, **V**, and **E**.

I hope this simple tool will be as helpful to you as it was to me when I first heard about it.

Let's build a more joyful planet for us all!

Bring the Grit Builders Together to Sustain Joy

"Vasbyt!" is an expression I grew up with. Literally meaning, "Bite down and hang on!" in Afrikaans (my first language), it is used as an encouragement on the sports field, or in real life, whenever adversity is faced. It conjures up the image of a dog biting down on a rope and hanging on for dear life with grit and determination, refusing to let go.

I learnt this the hard way when, as a young man fresh out of university, I had to become a soldier, as all able-bodied young white men were legislated to do back then in South Africa. During an intense period of three months, we were trained to become killing machines, able to withstand severe hardship. We were allowed very little sleep; we were constantly kept off balance. We had to run everywhere and were constantly and severely punished as a team, with extra physical tasks (like carrying heavy logs) when any one of us showed resistance or weakness. Slowly and steadily we learnt to dig deep and display the mettle we were made of. We learnt to work together for the sake of the group and not ourselves. We learnt the true value of having grit as part of our armour.

What I discovered during this period was that the most crucial part of this training, by far, was emotional and psychological. Once you could reach the place where you were able to ignore the screaming, the chaos, and your physical body pains, and instead focus on what was important, what needed to get done, nothing could touch you or steer you off course. You just needed to focus on what was most important and totally block out everything else.

Today, grit can be your super skill to propel you forward and help you outsmart your competition. Leaders and companies with grit move quicker, focus on what's most important, survive adversity and chaos, and earn a value and profit others simply cannot obtain. It is a huge competitive advantage, and it comes with a spectacular gift: once you master this skill—grit—you will be able to start living in a place of abundance, of sharing and supporting; a place where happiness and ultimately joy reside. Mastering grit will not only impact your productivity, it will be a joy game changer for your life!

In business and in life, we need to show this kind of grit from time to time. Some of us exude grit naturally; others have to work on developing this skill. And yes, this is a skill that can be improved over time. You need grit in your toolbox because it will allow you to find joy in life despite all the hardships that you will endure from time to time.

What I had to learn about grit the hard way can be taught through a series of training and coaching interventions. My work with individuals and teams has shown that if we understand how we can train our brains, how we can use powerful breathing techniques, and how we can control and reframe our thoughts to spend the maximum amount of time above the line, we can grow the super skill of grit.

Like the gritty farmer tilling the soil under the hot sun, we are preparing ourselves to become vessels to receive joy seeds. When we can withstand the onslaughts of the world, and when we have grit, we will have created the fertile breeding ground for joy in our own lives and the added blessing of spreading this joy to the world around us.

Chapter 2: Plant the Seeds

Master Your Emotions to Begin Your Joy Journey

Oupa and Ouma were not a typical married couple for their generation. For a start, Ouma was highly educated. Back then—in the very early twentieth century—this was exceptional. She left the district as a young girl to attend college in Pretoria, the nation's capital. She returned with a teaching diploma, and for many years, she taught at the local farm school, a tiny one-room building with only two teachers, close to the homestead. Both of Ouma's children, my dad and his younger sister, were first home-schooled by her before joining six or so other local kids at the farm school.

Oupa's education was much more limited. When he completed the equivalent of the eighth grade—back then in Dutch and English, as Afrikaans was not yet recognized as a language—his dad gave him a choice. He could continue with school if he wanted to become a dominee (a preacher), or he had to stop and join his dad on the farm. *Oupa* chose the latter.

What *Oupa* lacked in education, he more than made up for in his relationships. He was loved by all. His farm workers adored him. His trips into town would always take longer because of all the people he had to visit to do the farm business, visits that often were more social than anything else! The extended family was always welcomed with open arms by him when they came to visit.

Oupa was probably loved this much because he was not afraid to show his emotions. I saw him cry when he could not save a newborn lamb. I saw him mortally afraid when a bee was trapped with us in the cab of his *bakkie* (small truck) on a ride to the cattle—he was allergic to bee stings. I saw him exuberant with joy when the first raindrops fell after a long drought! With *Oupa*, there was always lively conversation, and I can still remember how he joked around with the farm workers who would bellow with laughter at *Oupa*'s latest quip.

Ouma was more reserved. She was stern. She maintained discipline. Her smile came less often. She was also very fair. We always knew we had to behave ourselves around her, or the finger of admonishment would come up to reprimand us!

Ouma crumbled, however, when *Oupa* used his humour on her and enveloped her in one of those bear hugs of his. She never could stay stern when *Oupa* pleaded our case with her.

They remind me of the second essential part of the toolkit that leaders employ—they constantly master their emotions.

This is not an area often discussed, and some people prefer to steer clear of the subject. Men like myself—of the age group I fall in (boomer, baby!)—are especially prone to using the ostrich response rather than openly discussing our emotions. We'd rather stick our heads in the sand and pretend that it is not happening at all! It is tough for us to discuss our feelings! This behaviour is also, unfortunately, not limited to people of my generation. It happens across generations.

Many men were also brought up with the belief that we're supposed to be tough and not show emotions. Growing up, we often heard the words, "Boys don't cry." That response is still hardwired into our male personas. Or cultural norms. It robs us from fully experiencing life. It ultimately robs us of joy.

While some of us are cut off from our emotions, others allow excessive emotionality to cloud their judgement, robbing them of their joy.

The art here is to find balance through curiosity. Something I encourage everyone to do, all generations and all genders, is become curious about our emotions. If we can better learn how emotions impact us, we can use these emotions to serve our best purposes. An informed decision, a managed approach, is so much better than a *laissez-faire* approach where you simply let things go and hope for the best.

When the COVID-19 pandemic struck, I was reminded of this. Many of my clients needed coaching in the areas of overcoming anxiety and mastering their emotions. All of us were on an emotional roller coaster. Many of them fell prey to this. There was lot of uncertainty and even fear.

In my coaching and public speaking, I love to use visual images and analogies. It helps people anchor their thoughts and get a clear handle on how to move forward. I started looking at how I could coach my clients to better work with their emotions—using their intellectual brains, along with curiosity—so that it would help them become masterful in this area.

This reminded me of my time as the CEO of a transportation company ...

I worked as CEO for a business owner who was training to become a small plane pilot. We used to take long road trips together as part of our work visiting a remote office of the company. He loved driving his truck and asked me to quiz him for his next pilot exams.

One time, he handed me this thick book on the theory of flying. It contained all sorts of terminology and interesting information. I was fascinated by how complicated of a machine the plane was, yet how relatively simple and straightforward it was to understand its basic instruments. The soldier in me was happy to see how important it was to have tight discipline with required procedures when handling the plane, especially when responding to what the instruments were signalling.

I had to think about how to organize the pilot questions so that over several trips, during a period of about three months, we could cover all the theory. I think I learnt more about flying small planes than he did in that period (he was driving; I was engrossed in the book), but regardless, he got his licence in the end, and all was happy and good.

My memory of the business owner and I working through the book on flying inspired a very useful analogy of the plane ride (representing out journey through life), the airplane itself (our beings or physical bodies), and the gauges (representing our senses, indicators of what was going on around us).

Using the plane analogy, we first focus on two gauges: the attitude and the altitude gauges, since they both closely link to the GritGraphic©. The same way the pilot interprets the readings of the gauges to get the plane safely to its destination, we can use the attitude and altitude gauges to position ourselves in our journey through our emotions every single day.

Attitude – Where You Are Heading in Your Quest for Joy

In a plane, the attitude gauge (also known as the artificial horizon) works very similarly to the concept of staying above *The Line*. You've probably seen this gauge before. It displays a horizontal line with a schematic of the plane

51

sitting just above or on the line. Like the pilot—who constantly has to be aware of where the plane is in relation to the artificial horizon line—you need to constantly be aware of where you are in relation to *The Joy Line* during each day. Are you going up, or are you coming down?

Gravity is constantly pulling the plane downwards. Pilots use their skills and resources to keep the plane flying forward. When it dips below the line, which is part of a regular flight, they have to be cognizant of it and work to bring it above the line again. They burn more gas. They adjust the flaps. They do what needs to be done.

The same goes for you during your day.

We all live in an environment that constantly pulls us below the line. The primitive part of our brains is hard-wired to be on the lookout for negativity and danger, to keep us safe. Therefore, there is this constant force pulling us down. We need to be aware of it. We need to constantly make sure that we do not stay below the line. You may dip below the line from time to time, but as long as you are aware of it, and able to bring yourself above the line again, all will be good in the end.

Like the pilot flying the plane is aware of where they are in relation to the artificial horizon line (the attitude gauge), we need to be aware of what our emotions are telling us when it causes us to dip below the line. If I start feeling overwhelmed, I need to become aware of it and commit to getting myself out of that feeling, so that I can rise above the circumstance that caused me to feel overwhelmed in the first place.

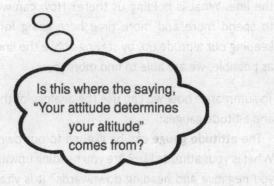

Is this where the saying, "Your attitude determines your altitude" comes from?

Altitude – Where You Are in the Moment Relative to Your Joy Line

The same way the pilot keeps the plane high enough to fly over trees and mountains, we need to keep an eye on our emotional altitude. Are we above the line or below it? If we are below the line, what is pulling us down?

It is normal and natural for us to dip down emotionally from time to time and go under the line. Everyone does. We can't be positive all the time! The key, however, is to realize when you are dipping down and not stay there. Like the pilot who will crash into the upcoming mountainside if they do not gain altitude soon enough, we will have an emotional meltdown or get stuck in a negative emotional state if we stay low for too long.

It is also important to be aware when we are above the line. What is holding us there? How can we use this to spend more and more time here going forward? By keeping our altitude up, by staying above the line as much as possible, we are able to find more joy.

To summarize how we can use the analogy of the attitude and altitude gauges:

The **attitude gauge** can be likened to our own attitude. What is your attitude like? Are you heading upwards, or are you negative and heading downwards? It is vitally important for the pilot to know if the plane is losing or gaining height. The attitude gauge tells them that. Our attitude is similar, but in an emotional sense. If our attitude stinks, things are not going to look up for us! If we show a great attitude, however, it will help lift us above the emotional thunderclouds of our circumstance.

Reading the **altitude gauge** in the plane can be likened to us determining if we are above or below *The Joy Line* at any given time. Like the pilot reading the altitude gauge to safely steer the plane around obstacles, we need to be aware, at all times, of where we are in relation to *The Joy Line*. Are we above the line or below? Are we high, or are we low? Are we soaring in the happiness zone? If we can stay there, we have a great shot at finding joy!

The third gauge we are going to look at is the fuel gauge. Although situated off to the side on the plane's dashboard, it is still equally important and should never be forgotten!

When a pilot flies and sees the fuel running low, they will always make a plan to land because they know if they keep going, it won't be good. To run out of fuel spells disaster.

They are either going to make a risky emergency landing, or they are going to crash. So, they always take care of themselves, their passengers, and their cargo.

For leaders—when getting too involved in every facet of business—we can become too busy and focused on the here and now. There are lots of things happening, all at the same time. We forget about ourselves, we forget about filling our own gas tanks so that we can keep going, and we forget to land. We forget to take a break. We stop taking care of ourselves and don't make the time for exercise and relaxation. We do not get good sleep. Soon we become irritable. Some of us may even have an emotional meltdown and cause irreparable damage!

So, here's the lesson. When you feel your gas tank running low, do what the pilot would do—land your plane. When you feel like your own tank is running on empty, when you get that tired feeling in your bones, when you struggle to survive through your day and your creativity leaves you, it's time for you to say, "Enough is enough!" It's time to find a place to land and refuel. Only when you do that will you be able to maintain or regain emotional control.

If you don't, your emotional crash may be just as ugly as the plane crash!

Anger – A Joy Killer Wherever You Are

The next gauge we can look at is the temperature or heat gauge. When pilots see this gauge rising, they immediately take action, as this is usually a sign of imminent disaster.

They slow down, drop to a lower height, and constantly watch the gauge. If needed, they make plans for an immediate landing.

We need to look at our own temperature gauge in the same way. Whenever we heat up, whenever we feel our anger rising, we need to take action. If we wait until we overheat and explode in anger, much damage will be caused. Instead it will be much better if we can take some time to cool our tempers down or walk away from the situation. This way we can make sure that our anger does not kill all the joy for ourselves and others.

I want to challenge you to think of your emotions as gauges in your body that you use to fly every day. If you are aware of these emotional gauges, curious about what they are telling you, and then able to act appropriately, you will be set up for success. You will be happy in the moment, and soon you will consistently start soaring in the joy zone.

Your Emotional Gauges – Indicators to Help You Find Joy

A useful way of looking at your emotions is to pretend, for a moment, that you are a pilot stepping into the cockpit of the plane and immediately reading the gauges on the dashboard. The difference is that you are stepping into the cockpit of your emotions, with your own emotional dashboard of gauges to read—each gauge with a story to tell, a report to bring. Like *Oupa*—who was constantly watching the sky for rain clouds when the dry season was nearing its end—these gauges exist to keep a tab on your emotions of frustration, disappointment, fear, hurt, guilt, sadness, anxiety, loneliness, inadequacy, and so many more.

Just like the plane's gauges give the pilot a warning—a trigger, if you'd prefer to call it that—we should be on the lookout for what negatively triggers us. *Oupa* knew that, when he saw that first rain cloud, he had to start plowing the fields to get the seeds in the ground on time, as the rainy season would soon follow.

We also should know how to react whenever we get an emotional trigger. When you feel angry, where does it sit in your body? How does it feel? What is it telling you? By becoming curious about the emotion—and not just getting stuck in it—you can lift yourself out of it and move on.

The same goes for emotions like frustration, disappointment, fear, hurt, guilt, sadness, anxiety, loneliness, and inadequacy. I always encourage my coaching clients to describe their feeling and how it feels in their body when they experience a specific negative emotion. When they can identify that particular feeling, when they are able to feel it rising within themselves, they will be in a position to act before it fully takes hold or they lose control.

I hear clients say, "It feels like a warm feeling rising up in my neck and onto my cheeks," when feeling angry. "I start feeling sorry for myself that I am not being treated fairly," when feeling inadequate. "It feels like a knot in my stomach, and I cannot catch a breath," when feeling fearful. When clients can explain what the feeling is like for them, I help them anchor that feeling and use it as a trigger next time they feel it.

What are those key emotional triggers for you when negative emotions rise up in you? Perhaps you've recognized your triggers from the examples above.

By getting curious about the emotion, you can identify and then discover how the emotion is serving you. Like a gauge on an airplane dash, it serves to keep you safe during your flight of life.

If you get angry, perhaps there is a threat emerging that you need to take care of. If you get angry all the time, perhaps you are not getting enough sleep or exercise, or there's too much on your plate. The latter may also be the case if you regularly have feelings of anxiety, or you may simply struggle with delegating. Whatever the feeling is, it contains a clue that you will be able to decipher, as long as you are in tune with your intellectual brain.

Understanding the cockpit of your emotions then becomes the key to your success. You are able to be happy in the moment. Soon you start living a life of joy.

A handy tool I use with clients is the Master Your Emotions tip sheet[5], by Nancy MacKay, the founder/CEO of MacKay CEO Forums. Nancy did her PhD in leadership and is a veritable fountain of knowledge in this area. Her words (*in italics*) are augmented with my observations and recommendations:

Emotions determine the quality of your life and emotions are contagious. Your ability to motivate and inspire the people around you will be enhanced by mastering your emotions.

---

[5] https://mackayceoforums.com/tipsheets/
how-to-master-your-emotions/#tipsheet

As we live in the present, in the here and now, this is also the place where our quality of life lives and our happiness is found. If you are a master of your emotions, you can use them to improve your current state, which influences your future state, as well as improve the people around you and the decisions you make. It is true that emotions are contagious, and as leaders, we have the added responsibility of our emotions and our mood directly impacting those we lead.

If the boss shows up in the morning all grumpy, pretty soon the mood in the office will change. People's behaviours will change. Hushed tones. Furtive glances. A place to watch your back and stay out of trouble will be the result. This will also have a direct effect on morale and how work is conducted. Client service and productivity will suffer, followed closely by the bottom line if this happens regularly!

A leader who, on the contrary, shows up with pep and determination, a contagious smile, and an abundance of energy, will have the exact opposite effect. So remember— when you are entrusted with a leadership position—you also have the responsibility of setting the tone for the mood of your team!

Seven Key Strategies for Finding Joy

Develop a positive-emotions mindset by applying the following seven key strategies:

1. *Choose positive emotions: love, happiness, optimism, determination, confidence, gratitude, curiosity, passion, health, resilience.*

   As we have learnt how to focus our thoughts, and how to constantly work towards keeping them above the line, we are now in the good position to choose which thoughts we want to allow to live in our minds. By choosing the positive ones, we allow our lives to be richer and more fulfilling, and we are left with a higher quality of life, more happiness, and ultimately an abundance of joy, all around.

   The beauty of this is that we can choose positive emotions despite our circumstance. By choosing these emotions, we actually become stronger as people and as leaders. We can resist any negativity around us, and we do not allow the negative emotions of others to infect us.

   This reminds me of a well-known passage in the Bible[6] (Ephesians 6:10–18) where we are encouraged to put on the full armour of God to stand against all evil. In this passage, Paul is encouraging the Ephesians to "... put on the full armour of God, so that when the day of evil comes, you may be

---

[6] The NIV (New International Version) Bible

able to stand your ground, and after you have done everything, to stand. Stand firm then, with the belt of truth buckled around your waist, with the breastplate of righteousness in place, and with your feet fitted with the readiness that comes from the gospel of peace. In addition to all this, take up the shield of faith, with which you can extinguish all the flaming arrows of the evil one. Take the helmet of salvation and the sword of the Spirit, ..." If we can do the same thing with the negativity around us, if we are able to put on a shield by choosing positive emotions, we become stronger, we can function well despite negativity around us, we are protected by our armour, and we are able to keep farming joy.

An important distinction to make here, with the choosing of positive emotions, is that this strategy should not be confused with the philosophy of positive thinking. This does not mean that we start treating everything in life as positive. We are not putting on a pair of rose-tinted glasses here! Negative emotions will still show up, but now we will have a strategy to handle these emotions. And although we will choose to focus on the positive emotions, there's no denying the existence—and the usefulness—of the negative ones.

2. *Embrace negative emotions: anger, frustration, disappointment, fear, hurt, sadness, guilt, overwhelm, loneliness, inadequacy. Every emotion serves you if you take action. What else could this mean?*

Emotions are like the gauges in an airplane. They tell us what is going on with our inner workings. They are there to keep us safe. It is essential to know if your airplane fuel tank is running low when you are cruising along; it is equally essential to know when you are experiencing feelings of inadequacy or stress. Negative emotions may just be telling you that you are not refilling your life tank regularly enough and that you are on course for a massive crash!

When we experience these emotions, it is important that we stop, breathe, take stock of where we're at, and then decide on how we can deal with the emotion by taking action.

The following simple three-step process serves my coaching clients well, and I've seen huge improvements in how they handle negativity while still keeping their eyes on the joy prize. Whenever you catch yourself in a negative emotional state, follow these simple steps:

Step 1: Stop. Don't engage in any kind of communication or interaction.

The Golden Rule is, when in a negative emotional state, your best bet is not to talk to another human being, definitely not write anything down, and for goodness sakes, absolutely not send an email off. You first need to identify the emotion, find out what it means, and then lift yourself out of the negativity before you communicate. If you process your thoughts by writing emails, simply do so, but you are not allowed to send that email before you've reread it, once you are back above the line.

Step 2: Identify the emotion, feel it, locate it in your body. Become curious about it.

By feeling the emotion, by not denying it, or trying to shove it under the proverbial carpet, you can become curious about it and find out how it can serve you.

An important technique I've learnt as part of my coaching training is that if you can feel the emotion in your body, it will be easier for you to recognize it next time it shows up. By physically getting into touch with where it sits in your body— that pain in your neck, that tightening of your muscles, perhaps that feeling in your gut—you will be better equipped next time to identify and deal with it.

One of my clients really captured this feeling well. When feeling sorry for himself, in a negative state, he described it as the feeling of a dark cloud that hangs over his head and face, staying there. If he stayed in that place, he would get stuck, and it would ruin the rest of his day. We spent some time so that he could anchor the feeling he would get in that moment. That way, he would be able to identify it and, before succumbing to it, become curious about it. What was the emotion telling him? If it was a gauge on the dashboard in the cockpit of his emotions, what was that gauge telling him?

He concluded that he felt overwhelmed and stuck. With this knowledge—moving him from the yellow brain energy of his emotions to his curiosity where he could unlock the creativity of his green brain energy—he was able to progress to the next step.

Step 3: Take positive action.

With the emotion identified, it is time to get up, take a break, sing a song, or go for a pee or something! My client learnt that by sitting there and wallowing in that negative state of mind, it inevitably affected the rest of his day, and he could even end up in a state of depression if he didn't do something about it. By taking positive action, he was able to work out his own plan of action that helped him overcome this negativity. Today, he recalls this experience every time he starts feeling that first dark cloud. He is able to let the sun shine through and chase away any dark clouds! He is able to bring joy into his life!

This principle holds true for all our negative emotions. By first stopping whatever we are doing, then identifying the emotion, then becoming curious about it, and then taking action, we are set on our path towards a richer life.

3. *Own your emotions.*

You alone are in charge of your emotions. No one can control your emotions if you don't allow it. I may offer you tools and encouragement, coaching and even cajoling, but in the end, it is your decision and yours alone. It is important that you understand this. You may have lots of people influencing your state of mind, some people may be able to *push your buttons*, but in the end, it is only you who can decide how this will affect you, your day, your life, your happiness, your joy.

Remember that you create your own emotions based on your interpretations. You get to choose whether you will allow a negative emotion consume you, or you can step out of it, learn from it, and move on to a positive emotional state; an emotion that will serve you well on your joy journey.

It is most important to choose commitment over hope. To commit to some sort of action, even just identifying the first next step, will set you up on your path of progress. By simply hoping for things to change, you leave too much to chance. Commitment brings action; hope brings no activity at all. It just leaves you vulnerable.

4. *Learn from emotions and move on.*

Emotions are fleeting. Although they are important and determine how we feel in the here and now, they come and go. It is best to enjoy the positive ones when they show up and learn from the negative ones when they rear their ugly heads. The important thing, though, is to then move on, by, for example, taking action to address whatever you've learnt from the negative emotions.

Don't avoid emotions. We have emotions for a reason. They tell us something. They can keep us safe. We need them to be alive and well and joyful. By simply avoiding an emotion, we miss out on all life has to offer. We may go through a difficult emotion, like sadness, but that emotion will bring us through to the next steps of our life journey. We need sadness, perhaps to reflect and recharge after a loss, before we can move towards happiness again.

Don't endure emotions. Emotions are there to serve us, but they are like the gauges on the dashboard—they tell us what we need to act on. If we simply sit in the emotions, if we simply stare at the gauge, we succumb to the negative undertones of the emotion, and it will lead us away from joy. Sadness endured for too long can become depression.

5. *Master your emotions by moving.*

An incredibly effective yet simple tool I've learnt is that we can use our bodies to help our minds change their gears. It has been proven that when you feel stuck in an emotion, you can simply move your body, and that will allow you to reframe and improve your state of mind. When you feel low, for instance, you should get up, take some deep breaths, and walk a bit. You will immediately feel an improvement. When stuck in traffic, force yourself to smile, take a deep breath (or practice some Square Breathing[7]), and dance in your seat to some music or sing your favourite song; you will definitely feel better, and you may even be able to let that guy—who just cut you off—get away with a smile and a wave, instead of a finger and an expletive!

When we are in the boardroom negotiating an important deal, or when we are being closely scrutinized in an interview, it is not always possible to get up and go somewhere or to burst into song! This is the time when you can simply use the technique of crossing or uncrossing your legs or arms, to signal to your mind that it is time to change gears. It is a simple technique, and it works. Give it a try the next time you want, no, *need* to change your emotional gears!

6. *Practice every day to develop a new success habit.*

Lots of ideas and recommendations were presented above. Each one, when applied regularly, can become a new habit, helping you along on your path to success. To tackle all the strategies at the same time will, however, be totally overwhelming. It is, therefore, recommended that you employ one per day and then start using it every day. Within a week,

[7] https://joyfarming.ca/square-breathing/

you should have seven new game-changing and life-enriching habits!

Imagine where you will be after a month, after a year ...

7. *Create your Top 10 List of what makes you feel good.*

I use this simple exercise in my workshops, asking my participants to simply list any activities and experiences that make them feel good in life. I encourage them to come up with at least seven in the first go-around. Then I ask them to prioritize each item on the list. If you have limited time and resources, which one will give you the greatest impact on your *feeling-good scale*? People typically list things like family activities, eating ice cream, listening to music, exercise, and the like. Once I had a troublemaker list "sex in the shower," to thunderous laughter from his group! At least he was honest!

After the workshop I send the participants off with two pieces of homework:

a. Revisit your list and rebuild it so that the 10 activities are ordered by priority. Call it your *Top 10 Joy Makers List*. Post the list in a prominent place so you can constantly be reminded of it. Make a concerted effort to spend a considerable amount of your time on those priorities. If your life is otherwise arranged, rearrange it over time. This is important. It will improve your current state, your day, your week, your year...your life! You will find happiness every day, and soon the joy will follow!

b. Discuss this list with your loved one(s) and ask them to hold you accountable to your list. Encourage them to develop their own lists and then start holding one another accountable. Work together to be happier together!

These seven strategies will serve you well if your start practicing them every day. Grow them as new habits to support you on your joy journey. By regularly planting your joy seeds, pretty soon they will start sprouting and filling each day with happiness. Over time, as you master the strategies, and they become part of who you are, your joy harvest will surprise you!

Five Key Areas to Prioritize to Enhance Your Emotional Mastery

Mood

Remember, you set the tone for your group in the way you show up. As a leader, this is an important responsibility you carry.

You can control your thoughts, which will have a major impact on your mood. By recognizing negative emotions, learning from them, and moving on, you will be able to improve your mood. By reframing your thoughts, you will be able to look at the exact same experience, which before would have negatively impacted your mood, and use it to actually improve your current state and your mood.

Adaptability

We are highly adaptable beings. Our minds are incredibly powerful. Remember that you have it in you to rise above whatever negativity life throws at you. Simply master these three techniques: firstly, focus your thoughts, secondly, live above the line by reframing those thoughts, and lastly, learn to master your emotions. Use these techniques to adapt and change as needed. Your quality of life will be enhanced. Your happiness will increase. Very soon your joy cup will start overflowing!

Stress management

When we are stressed, we are not at our best! When we allow negative emotions to linger, when we do not come up with an action plan to address that emotion, feelings of anxiety and stress are inevitable.

I believe that my stress is like a tank that life is constantly filling up for me. I work through the stress by exercising (running especially), singing, praying, practicing gratitude, and spending time on the top ten activities from my *Joy Makers List*. What works for you? I recommend you develop a similar system for your life.

Interpersonal relationships

We live in the here and now. We interact with people. When we show up with mental toughness, we are better equipped to build positive interpersonal relationships because we will not take things so personally. As a result, we will not choose negative behaviour, like defensiveness. Instead we will be open and curious. We will bring value to our relationships. We will support others better and become better at the journey of life.

Self-awareness

Being aware of what our minds and bodies tell us is critically important. When we are able to adapt and change to better suit (and serve) every situation—with full awareness of what makes us tick and what our limitations are—we will find ourselves on the path towards successful relationships (with others and the self!). We will be on the road to joy!

By becoming the master of our emotions, and by using our emotions to serve us and not control us, we start planting our joy seeds every day. We feel happier in the moment, and then very soon we spend the majority of our time in a state of happiness. As the seeds sprout and grow, soon we find ourselves living a more joy-filled life.

Chapter 3: Regularly Tend to Your Crop

Use Your Time Wisely to Allow Joy to Grow

Rhythms on the farm followed the trajectory of the sun and the passing of the seasons relentlessly and unquestionably.

When the sun set, animal and man settled down for the night. The chickens rested in the coops, the pigs were fed, and the cows were milked. Burning candles and lamps took away from scarce resources, so our after-dinner routine was quick so as to get everyone to bed promptly.

Before dawn, *Oupa* would be the first to stir to start his rounds. I learnt quickly that if I rebelled against the routine, I would lose out on some fun experiences. If I did not jump out of bed when he called, he would leave without me. Oh, the shame to be left behind with the others still sleeping in their beds!

I can still remember those morning rounds! *Oupa* would stomp his feet to break up the frost on the path as we left the back door. He would give me a welcome pat on the head and make sure that I had my coat buttoned up against the piercing cold morning air. His breath would make small clouds when he spoke. Our first adventure would be to try sneaking by the chicken coops to not wake the rooster. We seldom would be successful, and the crowing would soon begin, waking up all the lazy bones still sleeping in the house!

The milking would be our first point of call. *Oupa* had a small herd of dairy cows. There were the big black and whites we called *Friese* (Friesians)—in Canada, they are called Holsteins—and some Jerseys, the smaller brown cows with dreamy eyes. I can still recall how we could hear them mooing as they came up in single file, egged on by shouts from the herdsmen driving them up the hill into the holding pen. Once in there, some of the cows would drop steaming hot patties with a *plop* to the ground. *Oupa* would greet the men in their language. I can still recall their busy hands and the clicking sounds of their *Sotho* language (the local indigenous language) as they reported to *Oupa* about the previous day's activities and the well-being of the cows and calves in their care.

Soon *Ouma* would also be up to start breakfast and then meet her female staff to start the working day. The doors of the chicken coops would be flung open as *Ouma* let the chickens out into their fenced runs, where fresh water and feed awaited them. We would hear the roosters even when we were busy at the milkery. The day had begun!

Today, I am still an early riser; I'm most productive in the morning. I've learnt to jump at an opportunity before it disappears on me. I still remember the secure feeling and the joy I got from the rhythms of a well-structured day. Like *Oupa* and the herdsmen who had to rise early to fetch, feed, water, and milk the cows. Like *Ouma* and her staff who had to get the chickens out and get the breakfast done, so they could move on to watering the vegetable garden before the heat of the day. I loved the feeling of taking care of chores and animals, of being in control of my day, in time for the best results. When I feel as though I'm in control of my time, I feel happy and productive.

Where we are now, in today's world, the demands for our time have gone up astronomically.

"I just simply don't have enough time to get through my day!"

"I find it hard to keep up. There is no time to get everything done, let alone time to work on improving myself!"

"I'm constantly interrupted! My phone keeps beeping."

"I'm living on the edge of anxiety all the time. This needs to stop! Too many things are coming at me all at once. It used to be fun, but it's proven to be relentless."

Sound familiar?

These are some of the comments I receive from busy leaders in my workshops. They talk about this pressure all the time. Many seem to be trapped on this endless treadmill, and not only do their performances suffer, but they themselves start asking whether this is a life worth living.

Often, I would find myself in a state of anxiety when demands for my time seemed to pop up relentlessly and from every conceivable angle! I've seen some of my clients become stuck and transfixed on the *so much* they have to do, that they are unable to do anything!

The good news is that there is hope. Many highly productive leaders have learnt how to become masters of their time. We all have the same amount of time at our disposal, so how have these industry leaders mastered the use of theirs?

One of my clients, a serial entrepreneur running his own busy company and constantly merging with or acquiring competing companies (he prided himself on his company's ability to gobble up its own competitors!), was—despite all the demands for his time—always the picture of calm determination in action. Let's call this client Anthony. He was focused and determined; an example worth following. I asked him about his secrets.

This is what Anthony shared.

The Big Joy Picture – Focus on What's Important

Riding the Wheel of Life of Your Joy Journey: If you focus on what's most important in life and what your priorities are, it sets the scene for a life of balance—a life that can bring you happiness and sustain joy. Unfortunately, all too often, life gets in the way. We get busy with the here and now and get lured away to do what has become most urgent or, worse still, what is simply right in front of us claiming our attention. Typically, many of us start spending too much time working hard to be successful at a new job or business. We neglect the importance of the bigger picture, of those aspects that will bring us enduring joy.

I love using a simple tool called the *Wheel of Life* when coaching a new client (as a starting point) or when it is obvious that the client's life priorities are not aligning with work. It's simple, but powerful. I've seen lives changed with the Wheel of Life. For the better.

The exercise is simple. A circle (representing your life) is segmented into eight to twelve pizza slices, each representing an area of your life. Typically, these areas are Physical Environment, Career, Money, Health, Significant Other/Romance, Family & Friends, Personal Growth and Fun & Recreation. I adjust these segments according to individual and group needs and sometimes add segments like Spirituality/Faith and Purpose. This exercise can also help tremendously when coaching groups. It is, for example, part of the curriculum for the first retreat of a new MacKay group. It forms a solid foundation and helps to bind the group together.

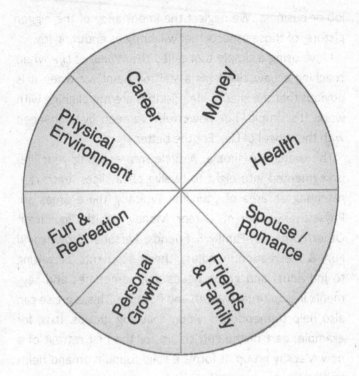

Once the segments are identified, the participant rates each area on a scale of zero to ten, where ten is the highest, in terms of how they are doing in each area and how fulfilled they feel by that area. Are they happy with their family life? How are they doing with personal and professional development? Is their career on track? By scoring each area, drawing a semi-circle accordingly, and colouring the inner part of that slice (a ten out of ten would mean the whole pizza slice is coloured in), the client's wheel starts appearing. This opens up the conversation. Big differences between slices will show up on the wheel, obviously causing a bumpy ride through life!

Once the areas of improvement are also identified, it is time for commitments. It is not good enough to just become aware of something that is out of whack, or even just talk about it. What is needed is some firm commitment leading to action. The clearer, the more concise, and the more compelling the commitment is, the better. I always ask for commitments right away, as that will drive the improvement and make the wheel move less bumpily through life.

As the ride gets less and less bumpy, more joy will be forthcoming. When you have a family life and business life in balance, there is more joy. When you have made your physical space prettier, and you work well with your money, you will have more joy. When you are developing personally and professionally, and having more fun, you will have more joy. When you are active romantically and spiritually, you will have more joy.

By focusing on the most important areas of your life, you will save so much time that could have been wasted on the less important areas. This will contribute to your time mastery—you are now spending your precious time on the most precious aspects of your life.

When identifying the areas that need work and then spending the time there, you will soon be like *Oupa*, *Ouma*, and all their helpers on the farm. They knew exactly what they needed to do and where they needed to spend time every day to make sure that every animal was taken care of and every crop watered. Soon you will find the peace of knowing that your big joy picture is being taken care of. You are regularly watering your joy seeds. Soon you will be overflowing with joy!

I received a cry of help from a leader—let's call him Jonathan—who was ready to quit his dream job. Even though I could clearly hear how tired he was, what was even more troubling were the undertones of panic; he was losing control. He had landed his dream job with the title he had always aspired to. As a general manager, he was now responsible for a big team, spread all over North America, and millions of dollars. At first, things were going well for him. He worked like a dog (his words, not mine) for long, long hours. He had racked up a new record of flying hours in order to meet his distant sales team members. Then more travel to see clients. And more travel to resolve issues. He neglected his family. He missed his young son, and his wife had become distant and withdrawn. There were more than 10,000 emails clogging his inbox. (I think he exaggerated quite a bit, but I let it go, as I believed it was due to his aggravated state of mind.) People were starting to complain that they could not get answers from him. He was constantly late for deadlines. His boss had become more and more demanding, and rumours were swirling that he was not coping. On top of this, he was not sleeping and could not remember the last time he had time to just relax. His dream job had become his worst nightmare. He was tired and ready to quit, which was really just him running away.

My first step was to get him emotionally stabilized. He needed some mental toughness! Our first session was just to get him breathing above the line and using his intellectual brain. We then did the *Wheel of Life* exercise.

We focused on where he was spending his time and what he was neglecting. After seeing his wonky wheel, it shattered his panicked focus on work. He decided to ask his wife for help—not only to help him get better sleep, but also to keep him accountable to his family responsibilities. He needed to get his life back in order to be productive at work again. He also decided to reach out to his boss.

It took a bit of time, but today Jonathan is happy and productive in his job. The dream took some work and is on track again. He negotiated a better travel schedule. He is home more. He mastered virtual calls with his sales team and with clients. He gets regular rest. His wife has become his partner in ensuring there is balance. Even their love life is back on track!

Living in Your Joyful Time-Saving Zap Zone: Way back when I was a young executive, a very smart leader introduced me to the concept of sappers and zappers. He was the CEO of a South Korean motor manufacturing company known for their creative problem solving.

He taught me that sappers are those activities or people that suck the energy right out of you. They may sap you instantly or gradually over time. You have to spend a lot of energy just to get yourself to do that particular task; it takes you out of your comfort zone and generally feels like a drag. When you are done, it is with a sense of relief, but you already start dreading the next time you have to tackle the same task. A sapper can also be that person who is just simply sucking the life out of you. That person who is constantly negative. The person who makes you feel inferior, judged, or frustrated. You do not look forward to their meetings. You feel tired, even deflated, afterwards.

Zappers, on the other hand, are the exact opposite. They energize you. This is the task on your list that you want to complete first. This is the person you look forward to meeting. This is the call that you cannot wait to make.

The question that the CEO posed was whether you are a zapper or a sapper. Are you zapping people around you with energy, or are you sapping the life out of them?

If we can spend more time zapping and being zapped, we will find joy every day.

When coaching, I ask my clients to make a list of activities that give them the most energy, to identify their zap zones. In the moment, these activities make you feel happy.

So I ask my clients to consider all the areas of their Wheel of Life and simply list anything and everything that first comes to mind. I encourage them to think about this list for a day or so, to let it simmer in their minds, to let their subconscious do its work. Then it is time to list the activities in order of importance. Which activity energizes you most and will bring you the most joy? Once they have their top ten activities listed, we start calling it their *Joy Makers List*.

I then get them to commit to discussing this list with those closest to them, encouraging those people to also draw up their own lists. I also get them to promise that they'll constantly, preferably daily, be reminded of their lists. Some post it as a screensaver on their phone or computer. Some post it on their refrigerator door or next to their workstation. The last step is for them to start planning their activities going forward. What are the areas that you should spend more time in? Which activities currently suck the living daylights out of you? Which can you delegate? Which can you stop doing?

The concept of zappers is very similar, if not close to identical, to your strengths. There are several handy assessments available online to guide you in finding your individual strengths[8]. If you know your strengths, and you know which give you boundless energy, and you start using those strengths to your advantage, you become unstoppable. Your enthusiasm grows. Your days become more fun and fulfilling. Work does not feel like work. You are happy. When you start sharing this energy with others, joy will soon follow.

Successful leaders have learnt the incredible value that is brought to you and your business when you surround yourself with zappers (of the people variety). If this kind of person is around your boardroom table, your meetings will be full of energy and fun—and ultimately elicit great results! If your sales team is energized and full of zest, more joy! If your customer care team zaps your clients every day, even more joy!

This brings us to the concept of success teams. We learnt that—if you surround yourself with people who believe in you, love what you do, and want to see you succeed—you, your career, your business, your life will start soaring! Work

---

[8] StrengthsFinder 2.0: https://www.gallup.com/cliftonstrengths/en/strengthsfinder.aspx

will not feel like work. When you're surrounded by people of this quality, you will be encouraged to do more and be better than ever before.

My challenge to you is to think about all those areas in your Wheel of Life, and for each area, think of the people who mean the most to you and exemplify these qualities. If you have a business, these are the very people you want on your board. These are the kinds of folks you want on your leadership team. Wherever you are on your journey of life, surrounding yourself with a success team—official or casual—will mean spending more time in the areas that make you happy and bring you joy. You will be better. Your teams will be better. Your company will be better.

Surrounding yourself, or better yet, filling your life, with people who are constant zappers, will constantly boost you with energy. You will be more energetic, stronger, and happier. You will get more done in less time. Work will not feel like work anymore, and soon your life will become filled with joy!

An Abundance Attitude Will Save You Time and Bring You Joy

Oupa, like all farmers, was a master of abundance. Every time farmers plant a crop, they're thinking of a bountiful harvest. Half a harvest is not an option. Farmers are in the abundance business. They harness all the resources they've got, get all the seeds they possibly could get into the ground, and wait for the rains to start.

If you are reading this book, chances are you have access to a myriad of resources too. You may not have as much as most. Perhaps you may even be in a place in your life where you have to be very cautious. But compared to the rest of the world's population, you probably have lots to be thankful for.

Or you may be in a place where you have tons of possessions.

Neither of these life conditions is important to the concept of abundance.

It is your outlook, your attitude, that's crucial. To have an outlook of abundance means you are living in a place of gratefulness for what you have every day. You may not have much, or perhaps you do; the point is you are grateful for what you have and readily share. You make room to allow others in, to take in partners and collaborators, or to simply let others share in your resources and opportunities. You believe that by working together and having a collaborative outlook, the proverbial pie can grow much bigger, and your slice will, therefore, grow as well. This is an outlook of abundance.

Farmers form or join co-operatives, so the entire farm community in the area can share best practices and prosper together. They build a bigger district—a stronger farming industry. Together they are so much stronger. They create and share abundance, and their lives become so much more joyful because of it.

The opposite is when, despite how much you have, you always feel as if you need more, you have to work just a bit harder, and you cannot allow anyone to come in and steal a piece of your precious pie! You believe the pie is of a fixed size, and anyone who comes in will take away from your share. You have a scarcity mindset. Life is an endless competition. You are constantly on a treadmill.

When coaching my clients in this area, I always ask them the question, "When is enough, enough?"

I recall a time when my wife and I were younger and our business brought us some success. At that time, we had two houses and three cars, plus many more possessions. We were constantly involved in the maintenance of these possessions! But it did not make us one iota happier having all these possessions! After all, you can only sleep in one bed at a time; you can only drive in one car at a time. The other car's battery is bound to go flat from lack of use!

So the bottom line here is not how many possessions you have. What's important is that you decide for yourself that you have enough. This will bring stability to your mindset. When you then start feeling grateful for what you have, and you start sharing it with others, your gratefulness will lead to "great*full*ness!!!" You will start feeling happy, and soon you will find that you are starting to live in a place of joy.

The happiness equation becomes really handy here. When you are able to adjust your Expectation (E), it will be so much easier to match your Life Condition (LC). Your formula will read: LC = E. By following the happiness equation, you will reach a place of happiness—that balance where joy flows from—so much sooner.

When you start living, and especially doing business, from a place of abundance, you will soon find yourself surrounded by zappers helping you grow the pie. Soon the fun will start! As you open doors for others, most will do the same for you, and together you will build a better tomorrow for all. You will do more in less time. By opening doors for one another, you all will become more effective with your time—you will all soon be together in the joy zone!

Stop Being a Perfectionist to Save Time and Enjoy Joy

A sure time-waster and joy-robber is when we display perfectionist behaviours. Sometimes we get so wrapped up in a task or project that we cannot help ourselves, so we keep working on it, keep improving it, keep perfecting it. We want to achieve 100%. Before we know it, other tasks and projects get neglected. Our productivity suffers. Our joy disappears.

The 85% Rule: It has been proven that, to take a project or task from 85% to 100% (perfection) can take up as much energy and resources as it took to get to 85% in the first place. This may be energy well-spent if you are sculpting a masterpiece to compete with one of Michelangelo's, or if you're working on a passion project where productivity is not an issue. But if a project or task requires being effective and productive, this is effort and resources not well-spent!

I coach my clients to stop at 85% and to fight the urge to keep going, trying to improve further. It is better to take a moment to breathe and admire and allow some space for joy to come in! After all, a task at 85% quality is something to celebrate!

When implementing EOS™, the Entrepreneurial Operating System[9], for clients, I love sharing one of the secrets to Gino Wickman's business success. In all his years of doing business, Gino learnt that it is more important to have all aspects of business reach 80%, rather than have some down pat whilst others are not quite up to standard. It is wiser to reach a certain standard across all fronts, than to be close to perfection in some areas whilst other areas are lagging behind. When you reach the 80% standard, it is time to stop improving that area and move to another area that needs to catch up. Businesses that follow this simple rule are more effective, more resilient, and adapt to change much better. And since businesses are made up of people, those people feel more in control, have less stress and anxiety, perform better, contribute more, and ultimately enjoy more joy.

Whether you focus to stop trying to improve at 85% or 80% is up to you. After all, these are not precise measurements. It's more of an attitude or value shift. You let go of perfectionism to be more efficient and grow a greater supply of joy.

---

[9] https://www.eosworldwide.com/what-is-eos

Ego Control
– Your Time-Saving Passport to Joy

We all have egos. Some are big, some are small. And then there are the loud ones!

Egos are there to bring us a sense of personal identity and help us navigate the world around us. They serve us well when strong enough to carry us through challenges. But when operating out of a negative emotional state, egos normally get very loud, in an effort to protect us from our insecurities.

I always coach my clients to show up with a strong but humble ego. It's a sure approach to bring you joy in the long run. Remember in life that it's not always about you, but you still need to maintain yourself and show up in a manner strong enough, so you can serve others and yourself. It's good to have a strong ego. If it gets big or loud, though, it is time to start asking questions!

My ego was tested recently.

One of my passions is singing in the choir. I get a ton of joy when, surrounded by my choirmates, we reach a place where the collective power of music becomes bigger than what each of us is capable of individually. A place where it feels as if you're soaring like a bird on the wing. Oh, what a place of utter joy!

Because of the COVID-19 pandemic, our church choir became virtual. Overnight. Our joyous togetherness was replaced by isolated notes hit in front of cold computer screens. Technique and musical giftedness became most important—areas in which I do not excel at all. I can sing well enough when surrounded by others, as we sing together, but I'm not good at pinpointing notes in isolation. It's just not my gift.

So I sent my video contribution in. I struggled to sing the song in the voice required, and hit the notes that were required, but I thought it would be acceptable.

I kind of forgot about it. *Then an email landed in my inbox.*

In a very friendly manner, I was advised that, although highly appreciated, my effort was not making the grade. It would let the rest of the choir down. The email came from our interim choir director, a young lady that I've noticed to be gifted with great leadership and musical abilities. Another millennial, a young man, equally gifted and the new conductor of our symphony orchestra, was copied on the email. Both had stepped up—when COVID-19 first hit—to take on quite challenging roles in our church music ministry. Both were quietly making things work. I had also quietly been admiring both of them and the way they had made their huge contribution.

In a very respectful manner, they encouraged me to redo the video, but it was also quite clear that I would not be part of the project going forward if my contribution was not improved. They outlined quite a few specific pointers on how to improve. Everything was there to set me up for success.

However, first my doubt set in. I felt like a failure. Was I even good enough? What was I thinking wasting everyone's time? I can barely reach the note when following the singers around me at church—what was I doing trying to hit these individual notes in a virtual space?

Later Mr. Loud Ego kicked in. "Why should I—a boomer old enough to be their father—have to listen to these two young whippersnappers?" *This problem is all due to COVID-19 and not being able to hear the other singers! It isn't my fault!* I thought.

I did not know what to do. I had a few days to respond and did not really want to miss this opportunity. I was stuck.

So I started to do some self-coaching.

What was standing in my way? Why was I even listening to all these thoughts of self-doubt?

I realized it was my ego. I was standing in my own way. I was only thinking of me, of how I felt and what I wanted. I had to look at the big picture. Why we were doing this in the first place? It was time for me to park my ego and get on with the task at hand.

So that's what I did. I followed the new instructions to a "T," did some practicing, said my prayers, and went for it. I hit the record button once again.

A day later, I received the sweetest email from these two great young ones. This time, the young man wrote the email, applauding me for improving and helping them make the music ministry better. And yes, my revised video was acceptable and would be part of our next virtual piece.

What utter joy! Not only to be able to sing, but also to be supported by such great young talent!

Is your ego strong?

Is it serving you well?

Does it get loud often?

Are you able to park it when necessary?

Hopefully my little story will give you clues on how to better work with your ego. With my ego parked, I could see that I had everything I needed to be successful. I just needed to get over myself. And I was able to reach a place of joy.

For egos, I often use an analogy I learnt from Mackay CEO Forums—the analogy of living in one of two houses.

The first is the House of Ego. In this house, the house of ego-driven leadership, you constantly want to look good. You constantly have to be right and do not admit your faults. If something goes badly, your judgemental attitude resorts to finding faults and someone to blame. You show defensive behaviour and cause others to be in the same mode as well. This is not a place of joy!

The House of Servant Leadership looks quite different. In this house, it is all about giving credit. If something goes right, you praise the person responsible in public and celebrate their progress. If something goes off the rails, you take responsibility on behalf of the team and promise to get it fixed. Respect is shown, and you accept feedback as a gift. You value other perspectives and act always for the better of the team. This is a place of sheer joy!

Are you living in the House of Ego or the House of Servant Leadership? We all find ourselves, from time to time, in the former, but by constantly working towards being in the second house, you will find yourself in a place of joy.

When your actions are driven by your ego, and you resort to what we call *ego talk*, you waste a lot of time. Not only your time, but also that of your team. By trying to be right, and not driving to find a solution to the problem, a lot of time is wasted. By triggering people to have to defend their positions at all times, the focus moves away from fixing what is wrong in the first place. Your team will stop bringing fresh solutions—ideas that could have made the operation faster and more effective. They will resort to simply doing their work and staying out of trouble.

As a result, more work will land on the desk of the leader. A bottleneck will occur. And we all know that operations move so much slower when there are bottlenecks.

Here are some phrases you will hear when a leader uses ego talk when speaking with a client (and the team) about something that went off the rails:

- "It was not my fault that this happened. This is Pete's project; he should have known better."

- "You are always dropping the ball like this!"

- "I told you this was going to happen."

More productive phrases, out of the mouth of the same leader would sound like this:

- "I am sorry this did not work out as planned. We'll get on it and have it sorted for you soon!"

- "How can I help to make sure we don't drop this ball again?"

- "We were worried this would happen. Let's learn from this and move on, but make sure it doesn't happen again."

By mastering your ego and eliminating ego talk, you will be able to move faster and get the team to support you better. Together you will be even faster. Soon you will be surging ahead to that place of joy where you are highly effective together!

Stick to Daily Time Mastery for a Joy-Filled Day

Ouma was relentless in maintaining the neatness of the entire homestead, including the house, the surrounding buildings, the yard, and the walkways. The entire yard was swept at least once daily. The house was dusted; the floors swept and scrubbed or polished. She had an eagle's eye for the hygiene of her kitchen (yes, it was HER kitchen), and also especially the *rondawel*.

Situated just behind the house, the *rondawel* was a round structure with very thick walls and a high-pitched thatch roof. It had tiny windows and was always cool. In winter, it was downright freezing! Traditionally, it had stamped floors, made of a mixture of clay and cow manure, and regularly polished to a sheen. The one on the farm, however, was a more modern version with solid concrete floors, also polished to a sheen.

The *rondawel* was where the dairy and meat were kept cool. The milk was kept in big cans that could only be carried by two grown men. The meat was hung off hooks, air dried, in the "safe," which was a square structure made of iron rods, covered with fine mesh to keep flies away. The structure also had long legs, so that rodents could not reach the bounty above, not that I ever saw any rodents near it. *Ouma* made sure of that! She was relentless in her war against any pestilence. I can still remember how she hated flies! She always had a fly swatter ready and commanded all of us to always swat any fly wherever we encountered one. She was our champion to keep us all safe from the diseases these pests could bring.

I was only allowed in the *rondawel* early mornings after the milking had been done, when the milk and cream were being separated. I had to wash my face and hands before entering (*Ouma* was there to keep a watchful eye) and had to make sure my shoes were spotlessly clean underneath before entering.

I can still remember the fun of working the milk separator. It had a huge round stainless steel bowl at the top into which the milk was poured. I had to crank the handle. At first it was slow to go, but soon the bowl would start spinning faster and faster! Oh, the joy of it! I can still remember the high-pitched *weeeeee* sound it made as it spun round and around. The heavier cream was separated from the milk and spun outwards by the centrifugal forces, where it was caught and diverted into an outer channel, to then be caught in a bucket below. The cream was thick and darker in colour than milk; sometimes even a light yellowish colour. I can still remember the smells and aromas of this experience: the coolness of the room, the steamy heat of the still-warm milk, and the pungent smell of the thick cream—it's all etched in my memories. I was filled with joy during this time!

Back then, I was just a youngster enjoying an experience with my grandparents. I was having fun without a single thought. Today I appreciate all the hard work and dedication that went into making cream in the first place. Without *Oupa* and his team's work, the milk would not be there. Without *Ouma* and her relentless pursuit of hygiene, we would not have a safe product to sustain us and bring the farm income.

This reminds me of my journey in becoming a master of my time. Without sweeping my proverbial yard every day, I could not keep my brain clean to react to new challenges. Without declaring war on the pestilence of time wasters, I could not assure that I get through my day productively and effectively.

Once the big picture is in place, and we spend our time on the most important aspects of our life, with the right attitude and surrounded by the right people, it is time to start focusing on our daily routines. What do we need to do every day to set us up for success to be able to find joy at the end of each day?

The Daily Happiness List – Setting You Up for Daily Joy:
From my own experience, when speaking with high-performing leaders, it has become abundantly clear that working through your day according to your priorities is the key factor in finding joy at the end of each day. It brings a sense of purpose and control. And if you can have mini successes and celebrations throughout the day as you reach milestones, it makes for a fun day!

You should start with the Daily Happiness List first thing in the morning, before you start working. It definitely needs to happen before you check your emails or messages. If you don't start with the Daily Happiness List, you will be distracted by the immediacy of whatever you are looking at. Before you know it, you will become involved in the first distraction, which will lead to the next and the next and the next and the next. Then your day will take on a life of its own, and you will lose control.

So start by making a daily list of tasks that need to be accomplished. Try to keep it simple and achievable, such as:

1. Write report

2. Phone client

3. Speak to staff about holiday pay

4. Follow up on financial emails

5. Review document

6. Clean inbox

Next prioritize the tasks according to urgency and importance:

1. If the task is both important and urgent, it gets rated A.

2. If it is important and not urgent, it gets rated

3. If it is urgent and not important, you nee yourself if you should be the person t it can be delegated, do so, but mak

person receiving the task is aware of its urgency. If it cannot be delegated, it gets rated B; keep it on your list.

4. If the task is neither important, nor urgent, it gets rated D and you really need to ask yourself why it is on your plate. If it can and should be delegated, do so. If not, it may be time to handle it differently. Consider letting the person waiting for this task know that you have refocused and will not proceed with the task. Perhaps a refocusing of your work or business is needed. If you decide to keep it on your plate, it gets rated D.

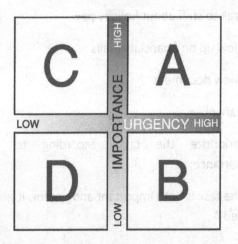

The prioritized list may look as follows:

1. D. Write report

   A. Phone client

3. B. Speak to staff about holiday pay

4. B. Follow up on financial emails

5. C. Review document

6. B. Clean inbox

Next start completing the tasks, focusing on one at a time: those marked A first, then B, then C, and if there is time left, D.

Focus on the task being done and finish it. Do not get sidetracked by interruptions, like phone calls or emails, except if they present tasks of higher priority.

It will give you a feeling of accomplishment when you physically draw a line through any tasks completed. It may look like the following:

1. D. Write report

2. ~~A. Phone client~~

3. B. Speak to staff about holiday pay

4. ~~B. Follow up on financial emails~~

5. C. Review document

6. ~~B. Clean inbox~~

When a task gets done, especially an important one, it's time for a mini celebration! Even if it is only a stretch break, or you just have five minutes to listen to a few of your favourite songs or drink a nice beverage, I do encourage you to make the most of the occasion. You can also be creative with your break; perhaps you will dance a bit of a jig when the music comes on? It will motivate you throughout the day to get things done. Anything that lifts your spirits, and preferably gets you off your butt and the juices flowing, will go a long way.

During the day, additional tasks will pop up. Prioritize them and add them to the list. Complete them according to priority.

Any tasks left on the list at the end of the working day go to the top of the list for the next day, ready to be prioritized with any new items.

Celebrate at the end of the day by looking back at all the progress you have made!

By making this a daily habit, you will feel so much happier every day. That is why I call it my Daily Happiness List. I have found that if I do not start and finish my day with this list, I feel like I am running from one task to the next the whole day. I am reactive to whatever gets my attention. I end up doing what is easy, and perhaps something that I should not be doing in the first place! Then at the end of the day, I am stuck with the most important or urgent tasks that I absolutely need to get done. It forces me to then have to dig deep and use grit to persevere. The energy that I bring to the task is not ideal, but since the task has to get done, there is no other choice. It gets done somehow, leaving me in a place of exhaustion or stress, with the knowledge that this task should have deserved better attention from me.

Once you have a Daily Happiness List, and you execute your day according to it, you will find that your days get happier. By sustaining this over time, joy will follow. By mastering this simple habit, you have opened the door to so much joy in your life!

I especially enjoy my little celebrations during the day. Oh, what joy they bring!

The Regularly Clean Inbox – Space Made for Your Creative Joy Juices: I used to have hundreds of emails in my inbox. Some were half-handled, some were opened but not really read, many were just floating around. I felt overworked and overwhelmed, and my brain kept coming back to many loose ends. I even dreamt about them some nights!

Why You Need To Clean Your Inbox: Since cleaning up my act, I've enjoyed many benefits (blessings, really):

1. **Feelings.** My feelings of being overwhelmed have disappeared. I am productive and on task. I feel in control. I have hope for a better tomorrow. I feel great! You can too!

2. **Brain space.** It is as though my uncluttered inbox has created extra space in my brain. With the loose ends tied, I have discovered the mental capacity to think about what's most important—the strategic issues essential to my business and my life.

3. **Creativity.** Extra brain space has meant that I can spend more time improving what I am doing and how I'm doing it. I've come up with new ways for improvement; these would not have been possible before with a full, cluttered brain!

4. **Productivity.** I've only achieved a daily clean inbox by implementing a solid system to handle the workflow at my desk. This has meant that I quickly get rid of the unnecessary items and appropriately handle the rest in an expedited manner. I'm getting more done, I'm spending my energy on the important tasks, and I've found that it creates more free time for me.

5. **Client Satisfaction.** My response times have improved dramatically. My clients get responses within a day. There are no missed emails and no emails buried somewhere in the inbox that get embarrassingly discovered at a later date! Not only has the timeliness of my work improved, the quality has as well!

How I Achieved Joy through a Clean Inbox: It all happened on a MacKay CEO Chair National Call. Nancy MacKay (CEO of MacKay CEO Forums) interviewed Colin Cox, a productivity coach, who is her colleague at MacKay CEO Forums. The topic was "CEO Productivity." I listened. I learnt. I asked questions. Colin was open to working together and helping implement time-mastering techniques. (You can listen here[10].)

I then read the book Colin recommended: *Getting Things Done* by David Allen. It is a gorgeous resource that will save you tons of time every day and has become something I regularly recommend to my clients to read.

---

[10] https://mackayceoforums.com/resources/podcasts/drive-profitable-growth-maximize-individual-productivity/

It took me five days to implement the system Colin recommended and work through the backlog in my inbox. Now I'm not looking back—the graphic you see below is a screen capture taken of my computer screen just last Friday!

All done for the day!
Enjoy your empty inbox

I now clean up my inbox at least once per week, at the end of the week. It helps me feel in control. All my future tasks are tackled, and I know I have a system that will ensure I see each email. And the emails can occupy my mind only when I need to tackle them. Until then, my mind can be uncluttered and free to do its best work.

The feeling is akin to having a "mind like water," a phrase Colin used in his presentation.

This analogy can be drawn from a pond of water. When you throw a small pebble into a still pond, like we did as kids on the farm, it makes a tiny ripple. If you throw a rock in, it makes a splash and a wave. The bigger the rock, the bigger the wave! Oh, how we enjoyed this activity on the farm! Soon the pond was overflowing and breaking over its edges!

The comparison here is between the pond and our minds (or inboxes). When our minds are clear and uncluttered, we are ready to respond to the tiniest *pebble* that may land in it—a pebble that may be vitally important. When our inboxes are clean, we are ready for every next task, big or small. If, however, our inboxes are cluttered and filled with rocks of all sizes, only the big rocks that fall into it can attract attention. They may not even be important! The tiny ones slip by unnoticed and disappear into the chaos of the cluttered inbox. Then we have lost control. Soon we start missing important tasks; we may even get a reputation of being unreliable, as our inboxes have become bottomless pits in which messages and tasks get stuck or simply disappear. With my regularly-cleaned inbox, I have found that I have renewed energy. With my uncluttered mind, I am able to think more broadly and tackle life more creatively. It has caused me to feel more in control and have more confidence, not only in my own ability to produce results, but more importantly to produce better quality results. It has become a source of peace of mind and ultimately brought me tons of joy.

It has left me feeling in control, relaxed, focused, and inspired by getting things done with a system to maintain the process.

I have become an advocate for this system, having Colin speak at all my MacKay CEO Forum groups. Many of my members have adopted this as one of their success habits.

By spreading the joy, my own joy got multiplied. It was especially heartwarming to see one member, who was struggling to get through his work, start showing up with a smile on his face, ready, and obviously in control of his time and his life. He could focus better. He could learn more. He was thankful for the intervention. His quality of life improved. His joy was obvious.

Do you want similar results?

How can you implement this system?

The Brain Dump – Make Room for Joy: Firstly, we need to make room for joy in our minds. Like a farmer who has to diligently pull out weeds that may compete with the crop, we need to create some space for growth. On the farm, when we pruned the fruit trees and cut out the dead and weak branches, the trees always responded by bearing bigger and healthier fruit.

We need to do something similar with all the weeds and weak branches of our daily lives.

We are bombarded with information every day. It is a simple fact of life these days. Distractions come at us from all directions. Add that to what already clutters our minds, and it starts to feel like we are on a constant treadmill of things to do, deadlines to meet, and people to please. Our

105

attention is taken up by useful and useless stimuli, and it is so easy to get distracted or to succumb to feelings of being overwhelmed.

We need to do a brain dump.

Start by finding a quiet corner in a quiet part of your day. You simply start jotting down everything that is in your brain at that time—those things keeping your mind occupied. Look at three areas of your life, such as Professional, Family, and Personal. Simply dump everything that is in your brain onto a sheet of paper or computer document.

Once you have done your first dump, it is time to look at the three lists below and decide whether there are some additional items you need to include on your brain dump list. The full comprehensive lists can be found online[11].

List 1: Professional and Community Contribution

- Projects started, but not completed

- Projects that need to be started

- Projects that you want to look into

- Commitments or promises to others

- Communications to make or receive

- Writing to finish or submit

- Meetings

---

[11] https://gettingthingsdone.com/wp-content/uploads/2014/10/Mind_Sweep_Trigger_List.pdf

- Reading

- Financial

- Planning or organizing

- Organizational development

- Administration

- Staff

- Systems

- Sales

- Marketing or promotion

- Meetings

- Waiting for ...

- Professional development

- Wardrobe (professional)

List 2: Family

- Family projects started, not completed

- Family projects that need to be started

- Projects—other organizations

- Commitments or promises to family

- Communications to make or receive

- Upcoming events

- Family activities with spouse, partner, children, parents, relatives, etc.

- Home or household aspects
- Health
- Transportation
- Pets
- Errands
- Community
- Administration
- Leisure
- Financial
- Legal
- Waiting for ...

List 3: Personal

- Personal projects started, not completed
- Personal projects that need to be started
- Personal projects—other organizations
- Commitments or promises to others
- Communications to make or receive
- Health
- Personal development
- Fitness
- Sleep

- Personal purpose

By going down these lists, you are reminded of what needs your attention, and you add those to your brain dump list. Your list may include specific items like these:

Professional:

1. Appoint new sales manager.

2. Follow up with client, Joe.

3. Write proposal for new prospect, Alan.

4. Plan audit.

5. Complete performance appraisals of support staff.

Family:

1. Plan Sally's wedding.

2. Plan visit to elderly parents.

3. Update will.

4. Schedule dog's vet appointment.

Personal:

1. Schedule annual check-up with doctor.

2. Find new personal trainer.

3. Read new book on sleep and improve sleep discipline.

4. Set aside time to do personal planning.

The first time you write this list, it will be much longer than this! Do not get discouraged. Every time you get back to it, the list will become shorter and the process easier!

Once your brain dumping list is completed, you can start building your control system.

Your Control System – Relentless Pursuit of Joy:

Taking Control

When we are in control of our day, it is fairly easy to have a good time, to find joy. When we're not in control, the opposite happens. We get dragged into less important "stuff," and soon we find ourselves becoming totally reactive.

It is important to take control, to step up, and take a proactive approach.

The first step in setting up your control system is to look at your "stuff" regularly and be ruthless in how you handle anything that crosses your desk the first time. A lot of time is saved if you can handle that item once and once only!

You first need to decide if the item is actionable. Does it need you to do something with it? Is this something that you should be doing?

If the answer is no, you have only one of three choices:

1. Delete it. (And be ruthless about it; get it out of there! This may be more than 80% of the stuff crossing your desk! We are bombarded with so much useless stuff these days!)

2. Incubate it. (For stuff that you may want to use later, or for hopes and dreams you may want to develop later. A useful place to incubate it is on a "Someday Maybe" list.)

3. Archive or file it. (If there is useful information in it that you may need later.)

If the answer is yes, it's something you should be doing, you first have to decide whether it has one or multiple steps.

If a successful outcome will require multiple steps, it is considered a project and should be broken up in the different steps needed to bring it to fruition. The first action then gets fed into the flow of your decision-making and handled with other actionable items.

For single-step actionable items (that now include the first steps of the projects identified) you have one of three choices:

1. Do it if it will take you less than two minutes.

2. Delegate it (and keep track of it in your communication system or on a "Waiting For" list).

3. Defer it:

   a   For yourself to do at a specific date or time in the future. Schedule the task on your calendar.

   b   For you to do as soon as you can. It goes on your daily to-do list.

A useful hint here, as far as archiving information goes, is to not screate a filing system within your email software program, but instead simply hit the archive button and file them all into that one giant folder. You can do this if you become a master at searching for information in that giant archive. Learn all the search terms as listed on the Internet (for the program I use, it can be found here[12]), become masterful at using them, and you'll be able to find what you need in no time!

Maintaining Control

Once a week, it is time to review your progress and make adjustments where needed.

The following three steps will set you up for success:

1. Get to a "Mind Like Water" state:

   - Collect loose papers and materials. Gather all accumulated paper-based materials into your tray.

   - Get everything to zero. Process all outstanding paper materials, notes, voicemails, and emails.

   - Empty your head. Put it in writing and process any uncaptured new projects, action items, those you are waiting for, those for your "Someday Maybe" list, etc.

2. Catch Up:

   - Review action lists. Mark off completed actions. Review reminders of further action steps to record.

---

[12] https://support.microsoft.com/en-us/office/learn-to-narrow-your-search-criteria-for-better-searches-in-outlook-d824d1e9-a255-4c8a-8553-276fb895a8da

- Review past calendar in detail for remaining action items, reference data, etc., and transfer into the active system.

- Review upcoming calendar events—long- and short-term. Capture actions triggered.

- Review "Waiting For" list. Record appropriate actions for any needed follow-up. Check off received items.

- Review Project lists.

  » Evaluate status of projects, goals, and outcomes, one by one, ensuring at least one current action item on each.

  » Browse through project plans, support materials, and any other work-in-progress materials to trigger new actions, completions, those you are waiting for, etc.

- Review any relevant checklists. Use as a trigger for any new actions.

3. Get creative

- Review "Someday Maybe" list. Review any projects that may now have become active, and transfer to "Projects." Delete items no longer of interest.

- Be creative and courageous. Do you have any new, wonderful, hare-brained, creative, thought-provoking, risk-taking ideas to add into your system?

This process reminds me of how the farmer constantly has to watch for and get rid of weeds in the crops. This is an ongoing and cyclical process. By regularly checking back, he is able to ensure that the crop alone gets access to the nutrients in the soil and full coverage from the sun's energy. When we are in a similar position and regularly clear our cluttered mind of loose ends, we will be able to have the "mind like water" experience, focus on what is important, and sleep like babies. What a joyful state to reach!

Reap the Benefits of Joy

Once my time-mastery system was in place, my joy levels skyrocketed.

I saw five huge benefits:

Feelings of chaos and being overwhelmed were replaced with feelings of joy.

I felt in control. I learnt to focus on one thing at a time—the most important one for that moment in time—and to do it well. There was a constant feeling of accomplishment and progress made throughout the day. In the moment, I was happier. At the end of the day, I could look back with a sense of pride. After a few days, I started to feel my joy increasing.

Brain space opened up; more room for joy.

As I started reaching that place of "mind like water" at least once per week, my brain felt more at peace, less stressed. I had new hope and felt like I could handle more. I felt rested. I felt ready for whatever would come my way. I was happy. Over time, my joy levels grew.

Productivity improved. Joy followed.

I started questioning why I was doing certain tasks. I reconsidered why I was doing other tasks in a particular way. I started thinking about how I could do it better, how I could be more effective. I stopped doing some joy-robbing activities. My days became happier. My joy levels increased.

Creativity skyrocketed. More time spent in my energizing joy zone.

I started having more energy to try new things. There was even time some days to hope and dream and tackle some of those items on my "Someday Maybe" list!

Client satisfaction improved. My client's joy became my own joy.

My response times to clients were diminished. My attentiveness improved, as my mind was more open and available to give immediate attention to important client matters. As I became more effective, the quality of my service improved. As I became more creative, I started showing up with more energy and enthusiasm. My clients started to notice and came back for more. They started telling others. My business development costs came down. I could focus more on the activities that bring me joy.

All of the above meant that I became much happier in the moment. Over time, my joy levels rose significantly.

I have become a real advocate for taking back control of our time. I have seen what reclaiming time has done for leaders I admire. I have felt the difference it makes for me every day.

Today I offer tools and tips for time-mastery on my website, free for anyone to download. I recommend Nancy and Colin widely, and I offer these time-mastery workshops in-person and virtually for groups and individuals.

I want all to enjoy the benefits and ultimately reach that place of joy brought to you by regularly watering your joy crop.

Chapter 4: Weed Your Crop

Cut Out Joy Killers

So what are the weeds that choke our joy crop? What are the killers that compete for our precious resources of time and energy?

They are the *joy killers* robbing us of focusing on the most important aspects of our lives.

Let's look at these joy killers and learn how we can cut them from our lives. Like *Oupa*, constantly watching his fields to find and cut out the weeds, we need to constantly be on the lookout to recognize and eradicate the joy killers in our everyday lives.

Cut Out Negativity to Create Space for Joy

A game changer that some amazing leaders employ is that they constantly choose happiness. There are two operatives at play here: (a) Happiness is a choice. (b) It is a choice that these leaders make constantly.

If you Google "Happiness is a choice," you will get millions of links. People are really, really interested in this topic! And it's no surprise, as this choice will not only determine how you feel in the moment, it will for sure change your quality of life if you choose to be happy.

One of the best quotes is by Rodney White. "We tend to seek happiness," he says, "when happiness is actually a choice."

To me, when you choose to be happy in the moment, the final outcome is not only a happy life—it ultimately leads to the much deeper feeling of joy.

In every moment, we can experience emotions anywhere on the following spectrum:

desperate pessimistic despondent **neutral** engaged optimistic happy joyful

←——————————————————————————————→

When we experience these emotions, it is up to each of us to decide what we do with them. If we choose to stay in the emotion, it will determine our quality of life, not only in that moment but also from that time onwards. For the negative emotions, I've learnt the best approach is to become curious and ask what the emotion is telling me. By acknowledging and then acting on it, I automatically move to the right on the spectrum into a more positive mindset. Learning from the example of the successful leaders, I can decide to choose happiness. I may be in the process of addressing something very negative, but by choosing the high road, I not only become more effective addressing the issue, I also give myself the gift of a happy and fulfilling life; a mindset that ultimately leads to a place of joy.

Let's say you open your email, and there's a message from a client who is very disappointed in some work you've done. Maybe it even feels like you're being attacked. First, find your feeling on the spectrum. Are you desperate? Maybe despondent? Then ask what the emotion is trying to tell you. You might get a few responses. You can even write them down. Make sure you are calm and getting good oxygen to your brain. Then use your curiosity to try to understand where the client is coming from and how you can handle this situation in such a way that you can find joy at the end of it. By being in a rational state, and not staying in the negative emotion that you first had, you have a much better chance at correcting the situation and moving on positively.

Are you ready to give yourself this gift? Are you ready to cut out negativity?

One of my colleagues is doing amazing work with gratitude. Steve Foran[13] offers tons of resources to get you living in a place of gratitude; a place that will definitely improve your life and help you find more joy! Some of the tools I use or have used in this area are:

1. Receiving Steve's "Daily Gratitudes" in my email inbox. You can also participate and sign up with him on his website listed below to have your turn at submitting your own gratitudes, to be shared with the people on his list. By regularly seeing what

---

[13] http://www.gratitudeatwork.ca/

others are grateful for, you will soon start being on the lookout for similar blessings in your day. Your focus will shift away from the negative to the positive in your day. Your joy will grow as you start realizing that there are many things every day that you can be grateful for!

2. Keeping a "Gratitude Journal." This can be especially effective when you use it to help you sleep better. An easy way to implement this is for you to—before you go to bed—think of at least three things you are truly grateful for. You can write these down and keep the journal on your bedside table. Keep them in your mind as you settle down. If you wake up in the middle of the night—especially if you wake up with the thousands of thoughts that can sometimes haunt us—your job is to start thinking of your three gratitudes again. Keep them in your mind. Be truly grateful for them. I start praying for more gratitudes! Soon your mind will settle down, and you will find it's easier to fall asleep again.

3. Beginning every meeting with every participant listing at least one thing they are grateful for. This will not only lift people's thought patterns to a place of optimism and possibility, it will also positively affect the collective thinking of the whole group through-out the meeting. It sets the tone for a great meeting!

Cut Out Relationship Killers to Find Team Joy

Teamwork – What Oxen Can Teach Us about Weeding Out Joy Killers: Teamwork on the farm was never more evident than when it was time to plow the fields.

Oupa was one of the last farmers to staunchly resist mechanization. To him, the tractors starting to make their appearances in the district were "From the Devil." I'm not sure if it was his resistance to change or whether he wanted to protect the jobs of his workers, but I can still recall him animatedly discussing it with his lead hand in fluent *Sotho* (a language I did not speak), so I could only interpret their expressions and emotions. Consensus was that tractors were wicked and that the old way of ox power was the only way to go!

What a glorious time it was when it was time to get the oxen *inspanned* (tied up)!

Weeks before—in the death throes of winter—*riempies* (thin strips of pliable leather) were cut, cured, stretched, and prepared from the previous season's cow hides, kept preserved in salt. These strong and flexible strips of hide were used to lash together the different components. There was the yoke (made from solid cut branches, sometimes driftwood found on the banks of the Wilge River that bordered our farm). It had to be lashed to the oxen's *skowwe* (shoulders). A strong metal chain was lashed to the yokes and led to the plow at the back. Then there was the long, thin yet strong lead that stretched from the two lead oxen to the *voorleiertjie* (front little leader, usually the son of the lead man) and used to steer the whole procession. Then there were also the whips—two long *riempies*, attached at the thicker end to short staffs and ending in a razor thin tail. These whips were never used to strike the animals. Their powerful explosive sound when whipped was used to keep the oxen going in the right direction. If one ox was stubborn, trying to break out of line, a whip would be cracked next to it on the side it was escaping to. The sharp sound would instinctively force the ox back into line. I've also seen it used when an ox stopped and refused to start moving. A few whip cracks behind the ox would soon scare it into movement.

When a young ox had to be trained, it was always first paired with an older ox with great attitude. This ox was always heavier and stronger than the young one and had learnt from experience that the best way forward was to follow commands closely and put the task and team first. To be stubborn, to try following one's own will, would just mean more noise, more drama, and a longer time carrying the heavy yoke. By trusting the process, by trusting the leaders and other oxen, and by doing its part in getting the work done, it would soon be time to enjoy the fruits of its labour.

The young ox was afforded every opportunity to learn and was encouraged to contribute by pulling its weight to propel the plow forward. Most of the young ones learnt quickly, but some took a bit longer. There was also the day when I heard *Oupa* mention to the lead hand that one particular young ox was just too headstrong and stubborn.

There was no point in fighting its bad attitude. I never saw that particular ox again after that day. The poor thing became *biltong* (air-dried meat strips, similar to but much more delicious than beef jerky) in a hurry!

Once the team of oxen was fully trained, it was time for the fun to start. And what a spectacle it all was! It took a lot of teamwork and noise to get them all *inspanned* and ready to go. It took a ton to get the big machine on the move. With shouts from the lead hand, and with the *voorleiertjie* showing the direction, the whips would crack at both sides of the two rows of oxen, and the procession would slowly start moving. I can still smell the dust that would fill the air as the heavy hooves of the oxen stomped on the sun-dried path!

The true joy followed when we reached the land that had to be plowed. Once correctly lined up and at just the right speed, the lead hand would shout out the command to engage. The oxen would grunt as the plow dug into the soil, snorting and pushing against the heavy strain. For a moment it would look as though the whole commotion would come to a grinding halt, but then the earth would slowly part as the plow started cutting through it. Oh, what joy it was to see the rich, red-brown soil as it came churning into the bright sunlight, released from the darkness below.

In the early mornings, the steam from the oxen's noses mingled with the steam from the fresh soil. It smelled divine, of fresh earth, of progress—the promise of the harvest it would bear. It was times of sheer joy. Everyone would be cheerful. *Oupa*'s cup of joy always ran over during these times.

Working with business leaders, I've been reminded of *Oupa*'s joy, when they talk about their teams. I've also been privileged to be invited by business leaders to be part of the joy in working with their teams. These leaders have been able to build a culture of high trust, and it is setting them and their companies apart.

If a team is together for a considerable amount of time, members get to know each other through casual encounters at places like the water cooler, the lunchroom, and social events the company may put on. Each time they meet, they hear a little bit more about one another's journey through life. By working together, they also see each other in action and hopefully build a rapport to work better together over time. This process of building trust in each other can take years and even decades to fully develop. This may have worked for previous generations when people stayed in the same job for most their working lives. Today it simply is not the case anymore.

Two factors came into play today: time and shorter career stints. Time is of the essence. We simply do not have the luxury anymore for a process to develop over many years. Competition is too fierce, and the business world is simply moving too fast these days. With virtual working-from-home scenarios now an everyday reality, the pace has accelerated even more. People also do not stay in one job for decades anymore. These days, most people constantly pursue new opportunities and will belong to a number of teams over the breadth of their career.

I've seen the pivotal work of two thought leaders become the go-to material for leaders to build a culture of trust for their teams. Patrick Lencioni[14] proved with his work that it is possible to accelerate the process of building trust in teams by overcoming five dysfunctions that teams naturally show. Stephen M. R. Covey[15] proved that self-trust and relationship trust go hand in hand.

Working with leaders and their teams, I've developed a series of group coaching/training sessions—interactive workshop experiences, really—to take a team from a position of low effectiveness to a place of productive joy in a relatively short period of time. We start with exercises and interventions to overcome the five dysfunctions of the team—the joy killers better known as:

- absence of trust

- fear of conflict

- lack of commitment

- avoidance of accountability

- inattention to results.

---

[14] *The Five Dysfunctions of the Team* and *The Advantage* by Patrick Lencioni

[15] *The Speed of Trust* by Stephen M. R. Covey

Cut Out Threats and Create a Safe Space for Joy to Grow

I've been privileged to lead sessions when the participants, even in a virtual space, are able to build a rapport with each other that allows them to overcome all five joy killers.

I've learnt that you first have to build a safe space for them to do this, and that you need to be the custodian, no the *protector*, of this safe space.

I start by laying down the rules. I use the following ten rules, calling them the:

Safe Space Code of Conduct

1. Bring fun!

2. Keep confidentiality inside and outside our safe space.

3. It is a privilege to enter this space and comes with responsibility to all the others here.

4. Take care of each other. Strive to understand, not necessarily agree. No judgement journey.

5. Be open and honest.

6. Stretch—our bodies, our minds, our comfort zones.

7. We will work in sprints and take short breaks to recharge.

8. Relax. Enjoy the ride. Trust the process.

9. We will make regular commitments for growth.

10. Spread fun, happiness, joy!

In this safe space, I've seen leaders volunteer to speak first, being vulnerable in front of their teams. I've facilitated heated arguments and showed teams that these are good and necessary parts of growth. I've seen people step up to the plate and commit to being better, taking full accountability, to bring their best results. I'm currently working with those same teams that are now blossoming and able to address all challenges that come their way. It has been an absolute joy for me to be part of this process!

Kevin approached me to help him with his team of brilliant engineers. Although they were scattered around the country, they wanted to improve their commitment and accountability levels. We decided on a virtual session, co-led by Kevin and me. I was the teacher/coach/facilitator and Kevin, knowing his people best, was in charge of keeping them engaged and challenged.

The value of this session was obvious during the interactive discussions, where almost everyone actively participated in the dialogue.

To demonstrate how teams can commit well, I led them through a virtual commitment circle. When we were done with the discussion, I allowed them a few minutes to decide what their takeaways were from the session, and what next steps they could commit to. Since the group was too large for individual commitments—there were more than fifty engineers—we asked them to write their commitments in the chat function. Kevin captured those commitments and could use the screenshots going forward to ensure follow-through and accountability.

Cut Out Disengagement – Sustain Joy in Your Teams

Commitment circles can work to cut out disengagement from any team, not only in business. Whether you lead a group of employees, volunteers, or sports players—any team, for that matter!—a commitment circle is a very powerful tool to get members committed and accountable to their peers.

But how does a commitment circle work?

This is how I lead a commitment circle:

1. Organize participants in peer groups. Peer accountability has been proven to be much stronger than any other.

2. After a morning huddle, learning or planning session, or at the conclusion of a meeting, get the

participants to stand up and face one another in a circle. In a virtual space, they are also required to stand (preferably behind a standing desk, or at least with their cameras at eye level). By standing it gives the moment a certain gravitas; it creates a ceremony, pushing them out of their comfort zones just enough to fully engage and pay attention.

3. Coach them to, one-by-one around the circle, highlight to the others what they have learnt, what their takeaways are, and most importantly, what they commit to doing. Stress to them that eye contact whilst making the commitment is paramount. (Note: Eye contact in a virtual space means you look straight into the camera lens.)

4. Once everyone is done, in a real space, the circle makes a collective high five to seal the deal, while in a virtual space, a virtual fist bump does the trick.

You'll be pleasantly surprised to see how this simple technique will give you, as a leader, higher commitment and accountability levels, ultimately driving results and the bottom line!

Natalie asked me to help with her team. She wanted to improve their levels of trust, and especially build their skills for productive conflict to drive results. At that stage, her team was so sensitive to the concept that they did not even want to use the word "conflict." I had to use the word "disagreement."

Natalie is a well-established and experienced leader with incredible self-awareness. Because she was not afraid to be vulnerable in front of her team, we could use it to accelerate the speed at which the trust could grow during the sessions. By the third session, we were both happy to see young and old, from different cultures and experiences, working bravely together to address issues and challenges. Once they understood each other better from listening to one another's life stories and taking into account their personal and conflict style preferences, they surprised us by how they stepped up to the plate to form a tight team, grounded in respect and trust.

Natalie reported a few months after the sessions that what they had learnt had become part of their culture and had accelerated their results. She recently invited me back to do further work with her team. I am still working with them today.

Business leaders I've worked with have reported that a culture of high trust brings several benefits, including:

Savings. More trust means less dependence on written agreements and procedures, contracts, and the like. Accountants and auditors have less work. Lawyers are seldom, if ever, needed. These costs come way down or disappear.

Speed. Decisions are quickly made. Team members get what they need without delay and can move promptly to get results expeditiously. Negotiations are swift. The company becomes nimble, quickly reacting to a changing environment. Being first to market, means you can set higher prices and keep beating the competition. Soon you become an industry leader or disruptor.

Profits. With speed up and costs down, the bottom line grows. More profit means more opportunity for the company, to invest in your people and to keep building your trust culture.

A stronger company. With higher trust, decision-making speeds up, resulting in faster transactions. Products get to customers faster. Costs come down, as controls can be simplified. Higher turnover and lower costs mean a better bottom line. Management and staff running the company in a high trust environment makes it more attractive to investors.

These are certainly great outcomes. It makes the investment of time and resources in building the culture a no brainer. That's partly why I so much enjoy doing this work. The real joy, however, comes when you speak with the employees of these companies. You should hear them! You should see their faces when they speak about the difference it has made in their lives!

They mention things like the following:

Safety. Team members feel safe. They have each other's backs and feel safe to speak their minds with respect. Team members can be open without fear of discrimination or retribution. Feedback is part of the culture.

Openness. Communication flows freely. Everyone knows why the team is there, what it needs to do, and where it's headed. There are no secrets and difficult conversations happen naturally when they are needed.

Happier Employees. They have a good place to work. They have each other's backs. There is permission to fail and improve. You see smiles and friendly humour. They encourage and hold one another accountable. Their morale is sky high!

Happier Customers. Customers learn that what sets this company apart is that it delivers on its promises, fast and effectively. They love working with happy employees who constantly want feedback to improve how they serve their customers.

Whether we are on the farm working with a team of oxen, in the boardroom with a team of executives, or on the sports field with a team of athletes, these principles hold true. It is possible to annihilate those joy killers that hamper relationships and wreck the team. The joy killers are called absence of trust, fear of conflict, lack of commitment, avoidance of accountability, and inattention to results. It is possible to weed them all out of your team, and in a relatively short time, start enjoying the fruits of your labour.

Chapter 5: Harvest

Reap the Benefits of Joy by Living Your Purpose

A final game changer that amazing leaders employ is they know their *sweet spot* and actively live their purpose. To see them leading in this way reminded me of one huge event on the farm every year, when so many people had to work together, each bringing their skills to the table, each working towards getting the collective job done. It was when the wool had to come off!

Sheep shearing season was a time of great activity on the farm. Everyone had a job, a purpose.

Weeks before the shearing team would arrive, preparations would start. The big barn had to be cleaned from top to bottom. The wagon, parked in the barn, would get a scrubbing–this is where the team would be sleeping. Ropes were flung across the beams, from which the big square hessian bags were suspended to form huge cubes hanging a foot or so above the clean swept floor. This is where the wool would go. A couple of big tables, on which the wool would be classed, were placed along the side with the best light.

Ouma and the female staff were busy preparing meals. The big coal stove was running non-stop. The kitchen, the larder, and *rondawel* were a frenzy of activity. Pots and pans were clanging, the fire was being stoked, *Ouma* was directing traffic, and vegetables and fruit were being peeled. Some extra chickens and meat lambs ended up on the butcher's block to make sure there was enough solid meals for everyone. The big, black, heavy, round, three-legged cast iron pots were being scrubbed and oiled, ready for the fires that were set next to the barn where the meals would be cooked.

The sheep, heavily laden with their load of fleece, were quite uncomfortable by this time. What had protected them against the cold of the winter months and attacks from predators, like the roaming jackals, had made them ungainly in movement and caused them to overheat easily. They were gently shepherded from the hills to holding pens behind the big barn during the cool hours of the morning. I recall their bleating and their stupid behaviour. These were not the most intelligent of beings! The shepherds and the dogs had their hands and paws full to keep them on track. It only took one sheep to take a wrong turn for the whole lot to, err, sheepishly follow suit. I understood then why there are so many sayings involving sheepish behaviour!

Oupa took the opportunity to do a head count. As the sheep came down into the holding pens, he had them come through a narrow passage to form single file and easily be counted. Although he was not an educated man and had his limits as far as math went, he had his own system! On the back of a cigarette box, he would count each passing sheep, one after the other until he had four lines in a row. The fifth sheep's line would go diagonally across the first four lines, forming the first group of five. And so on.

When the count was done, *Oupa* would carefully transfer it to his notebook. He would then multiply the number by five (sometimes using long multiplication; he showed me proudly) and then add any additional single sheep that were not enough to form a group of five. I recall he would have in the region of 200 groups, for a total of more than 1,000 sheep. It was a lot of sheep for those years! These numbers would then carefully be transferred, with the date, to his notebook. *Oupa* kept a little notebook in his shirt's breast pocket, with a short pencil that he sharpened with his pocketknife that was always with him. He would always lick the pencil's lead point. It would make the writing more permanent, he would claim.

What a joyous day it was when the shearing team arrived. A group of about five strong, young *Sotho* (a local tribe) men brought extra energy to an already invigorated homestead! They would sharpen their shearing scissors with little squirts from the oil cans on the *slypstene* (flat grindstones made of local sandstone) and test the blades' smoothness by narrowing their eyes when holding it into the sun–it would reflect the light from its sharp, silver edge. Some would inspect the sheep and plan with *Oupa* which sheep should come through first. Then the men's clicking sounds would start, heralding in the spectacle of the rebirth of the sheep!

The first sheep would come in, egged on by its shepherd. The shearer would expertly grab it by a hind leg, then flip it onto its butt, with its backside cradled between his legs. As soon as the sheep was docile, the clicking sound of the shears would start. With deft cuts around the wrists and ankles, he would start opening the whole sheaf. Like the unbuttoning of a coat, the *snip, snip, snip* of the shears would release the lily-white sheep from its brown winter coat.

Oh what joy! The released sheep, naked in its whiteness, would stand still for a second. Then the sensation of the cool passing breeze over its body, the lightness of its limbs without the heavy burden it was carrying, would register. It would make a first leap of joy! Bounding around, bleating like stupid sheep can, it would be a sight to see!

It reminds me now, that, in business and life, we need to have many, many systems in place and people working together to reach such a place of utter joy. Like the sheep that needed a gentle hand when it was burdened, we need guides and mentors and leaders to lead us. Like the expert shearers, we need specialists to do for us what they do best. Like *Ouma*'s team of women, we need a supportive structure to set us up for success.

Everyone on the farm knew what their purpose was and that it was essential. They knew that if they dropped the ball, someone else would be left in a lurch. There was inherent trust in one another, in the leaders and the systems in place.

Your Purpose Statement – Unlock Your Joy

In business it is essential—in order to find success similar to that of the people making sheep shearing on the farm successful—that we know what our purpose is, and how it relates to the purpose of the business venture. I have found the Entrepreneurial Operating System (EOS™)[16] to be very useful here. This powerful system, based on five books[17], brings together many thought leaders and their work in one very simple yet comprehensive system that addresses all aspects of business, including strategy and people. It introduces the concept of finding your *sweet spot* in business—a concept that helps you find your purpose.

The analogy that can be used here is that of an athlete hitting a ball on the sports field. It may be baseball. It may be cricket. Tennis. Or pickleball. Every player knows that feeling when they hit their proverbial *sweet spot*. In that moment, when you hit the ball with just the right amount of force, at just the right angle in exactly the right place, the ball flies off sweetly and further than ever before. There sometimes is a sweet sound, like a *zing*, at the very moment of contact, and you are able to feel it in your hands and arms. It just feels right. In baseball, that ball would fly out of the park! It is a thing of beauty and joy!

---

[16] https://www.eosworldwide.com/

[17] *Traction* by Gino Wickman, *Good to Great* by Jim Collins, *The Four Obsessions of an Extraordinary Executive* by Patrick Lencioni, *How To Be A Great Boss* by Gino Wickman and René Boer, and *The Five Dysfunctions of a Team* by Patrick Lencioni

That moment of impact, when the ball strikes the bat, is akin to the moment of contact when the client is served in business. If the ball is not sweetly struck, when it, for example, glances off the bat and goes up into the air, the opposing players (or the competitors in business) get the opportunity to take the batter out. If the batter misses the ball altogether, there is no opportunity to score. If this happens three times in a row, the batter is taken out, failing their team.

It is very similar to business.

However, when the ball is sweetly struck, it is altogether a different outcome! The batter's team is in play. They can move around the bases and score runs! A new batter gets the opportunity to come in and serve the team. All the competition can do is defend. Sometimes, if it is hit straight out of the park, all the competition can do is watch!

Before exploring this baseball analogy—this joyful moment when the *sweet spot* is hit—to make it better applicable to business, we need to hear the fable of the hedgehog and the fox. It is an important tool to help people get to that aha moment when they get closer to discovering how they can hit the *sweet spot* time after time.

It is a simple tale, simply told. It is very powerful. The question is:

Are you a hedgehog or a fox?

Isaiah Berlin's tale divided the world into hedgehogs and foxes, based upon an ancient Greek parable, "The fox knows many things, but the hedgehog knows one big thing." The fox is very cunning and able to come up with many complex strategies for sneak attacks upon the hedgehog. Every day the fox circles the hedgehog's den, waiting for the perfect moment to pounce. Fast, sleek, beautiful, fleet of foot, and crafty—the fox looks like the sure winner. The hedgehog, on the other hand, is a dowdier creature, looking like a genetic mix-up between a porcupine and a small armadillo. He waddles along, going about his simple day, searching for lunch and taking care of his home.

The fox decides to wait in ambush at an open spot in the forest. The hedgehog, minding his own business, wanders right into the trap. *Aha, I've got you now*, thinks the fox. He leaps out, bounding across the ground, fast as a flash! The hedgehog, hearing the fox approach, looks up and thinks, *Here we go again. Will he ever learn?* The hedgehog rolls himself into a perfect little ball, the way hedgehogs do, and becomes a ball of sharp, impenetrable spikes. The fox, bounding towards his prey, sees the hedgehog's defence and has to stop and beat the retreat.

Back in the forest, the fox begins to calculate a new line of attack. Each day, some version of this battle between the hedgehog and the fox takes place, and despite the greater cunningness of the fox, the hedgehog always wins.

Berlin uses this tale as an illustration to divide people into two basic groups: foxes and hedgehogs. Foxes pursue many things, all at the same time. They see the world in all its complexity. Their thinking is often scattered and unfocused. They find it difficult to focus on one concept or vision. Hedgehogs, on the other hand, simplify complexity into a single organizing idea—a basic principle or concept that brings focus and direction. It doesn't matter how complex the world is, a hedgehog translates all challenges and dilemmas to simple—indeed almost simplistic—hedgehog ideas. For a hedgehog, anything that does not serve the hedgehog holds no relevance.

I've seen successful business leaders know exactly what they need to do and when to do it, to hit the *sweet spot* in business. But how do they know? Let's return to the baseball analogy and do some discovering.

EOS™ uses a powerful graphic of a ball. The same ball that needs to be hit exactly right to make it fly out of the park.

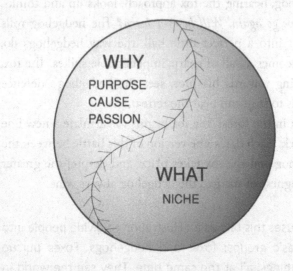

If you have ever handled a baseball, you may have noticed that it is made up of two pieces of material, two pieces of exactly the same form, stitched together, each covering half of the surface area of the ball. The one half, on the left in our graphic, is compared to the why of the company or the individual. Aspects like the purpose, the cause, and the passion (P/C/P) need to be unpacked.

The first thing we want to know is your "Why."

Why are you in business? Why are you personally on this planet?

I ask people three simple questions to ponder here:

1. Why are you (or your company) on this planet?

2. Who are you on this planet for?

3. What impact do you want to have?

The second part, your "What" or niche, is where we discover what you are bringing and whom you are bringing it to.

Your "Why" and your "What" combined determines you or your company's *sweet spot*—a powerful concept. Also called your core focus, your mission statement, voice, hedgehog concept, or unique ability, it is that area where there is agreement between your P/C/P and your niche.

The objective here is for participants to develop their own purpose statements. To help them reach a place of greater understanding, to discover their highest aspirations and what they believe is most important in their lives, I get them to answer the following questions:

1. What do you value most in life? What is most important to you?

2. What do you really like to do at work? What gives you energy?

3. What do you really like to do in your personal life? What inspires you?

4. What are your natural talents and gifts?

5. What are your greatest goals and desires?

I ask them to list three to five things for each question. The answers are intended to provide greater insight and clarity.

EOS™ goes a step further. It does not stop at personal purpose only. It also asks what your cause and your passion are. I ask participants to bear this in mind when completing their questions.

Then I give them some examples of personal purpose statements and time to ponder their own personal purpose statements. I encourage them to look at where their passion and their giftedness come together, as purpose is defined as the place where passion and giftedness come together.

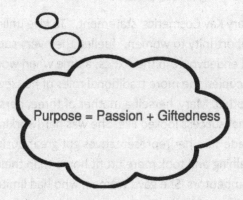

Purpose = Passion + Giftedness

Some examples of personal purpose statements:

- "To enjoy the freedom of choice and to add value to the lives of people in my life."

- "To inspire business leaders to make a huge impact on the world."

- "To be joy-filled! To inspire others to find joy in their personal, professional, and spiritual lives."

- "To inspire people to protect the planet through inspirational and educational movies that I produce."

- "To help create a business profit that achieves our social purpose."

With all three aspects of your "Why" considered—namely purpose, cause, and passion—we have covered the first half of reaching the *sweet spot*.

Some business examples here can help us determine our own personal purpose statements.

- Mary Kay Cosmetics' statement, "To give unlimited opportunity to women," fuelled their very successful endeavours in the sixties, a time when women occupied the more traditional roles of housewife and mother. Mary, herself a mother of three, personified what success looked like. She was hardworking and made sure her representatives got great business training and took more profit home than their competitors. She gave women, who had limited opportunities, a business model where they could sell cosmetics during house parties and establish their own businesses In the United States. She lifted people out of poverty with this model, but it did so much more. Although women were selling cosmetics to make money, Mary was helping them find opportunities in life that were not available to them otherwise.

- Disney's statement, "To make people happy," is very simple and easy to understand. Disney stories have happy endings. I know when watching a Disney movie that the heroes are going to win in the end. They may have the odds stacked against him, but I know they're going to get there in the end, and the bad guys are going to lose—it's Disney, so you can relax. When you go to a Disney resort, you know that everything and everyone there will make you happy. It's smiles. It's happy music. It's a break from the serious world outside. In the meantime, Disney takes all your money. They send you home with a huge credit card bill. They're reaching all their financial goals and you are okay with it because they've made you and your family happy, and in the end, we all want to be happy.

- I particularly like Nike's statement, "To experience the emotion of competition, winning, and crushing competitors." We all have seen athletes on the world stage compete with the Nike swoosh on their outfits. We all have seen them crush their competition. When we—ordinary mortals like me who will never be of that same standard—go out for a run or training session, we put on our Nike attire, and we feel a bit of that same emotion. For a moment, we can all feel like a champion, even though we may only be competing against ourselves. It is a powerful motivator.

When working with individuals or groups, I encourage them to start playing with words, phrases, and concepts that can describe their own purpose/cause/passion statements. We are looking for statements describing the following:

1. It is your reason for being.

2. It comes from your heart and involves everyone.

3. It is not about money. It is beyond money.

4. It is big and bold, much bigger than a goal.

5. It ignites passion.

6. It is short at three to seven words, described in accessible language that everyone can understand.

7. It has an "aha" effect.

I ask participants the question:

What is your purpose/cause/passion?

I then encourage them to write down key words and concepts, short phrases, and ideas. I enforce time pressure, so that they will jot down the first ideas that come into their minds. Then I encourage them to start stringing the words together and come up with a draft statement. It may still be rough at that time, and that is okay. I ask them to share their draft statements in a roundtable discussion. It helps them when they have to verbalize what they have written. It also inspires them to keep working when they hear what their peers are coming up with.

I also share with them my P/C/P statement:

> *We are joy farmers. We believe we are not alone. We inspire joy in leaders, to pass it on to their teams, to their clients, resulting in more profits to be able to share more joy. Joy all around, that's what we're all about!*

At this stage, I emphasize to them that this is just the first step in them discovering their P/C/P statements. I encourage them to keep working on it over time and to refine it as they go forward.

Then we move forward and start looking at our niches.

Your Niche – Pinpoint Your Joy

It is fabulous to know what your purpose is and to have your P/C/P all figured out. It brings you joy every day when you work purposefully, along with the passion it brings you. In order to take it to the next level though, and to make you more competitive, you also need to figure out what your niche is.

I, therefore, ask participants to consider what they think they can do better than anyone else, what their superior skill is. I encourage them to find something simple. Simplicity can bring focus and clarity. Orville Redenbacher said, "Do one thing ..." and made it their total focus. That *thing* was popcorn, and even though they may do some things that are not directly related to popcorn, it always has to be connected to their central focus: popcorn. When, as an example, they started working with chocolate, it was only to develop chocolate coverings or dips for their popcorn. They did not go into exclusive chocolate lines and diluted their single-minded focus on their popcorn niche. This makes their brand the first one millions of people think of when they want popcorn. This is why they could, over time, become the world leader in anything related to popcorn.

It reminds me of an individual who knows what their strengths and weaknesses are, and by focusing on their strengths, over time, they become excellent at it, setting them apart from competitors. But take it a step further. If you can ascertain what your one strength is, that passion that energizes you and does not feel like work, and develop it into a superior skill, it can set you apart and bring you tons of joy! That is called your niche.

So the question is:

What can you do better than anyone?

At this stage, I ask the participants to again jot down thoughts and ideas to describe their niche. I ask them to think about how the Orville Redenbacher example can help them.

Once they have some thoughts down, I ask them to share. Again, I emphasize to them that this is just the first step.

Your Sweet Spot – When Joy Flows Effortlessly

Now we come to the real challenge. It is time to put the two pieces of work together and combine them into one *sweet spot* statement.

We are looking for that place where there is agreement and focus on your P/C/P statement and your niche. This is where three areas intersect: what you are passionate about, what you can be the best in the world at, and what drives your economic engine.

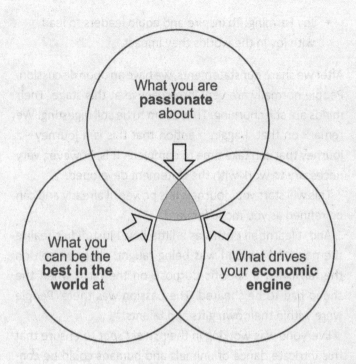

I ask participants to look at their personal purpose statement, their business P/C/P statement, and their niche, and then come up with a simple statement that combines these all.

Some examples:

- Walgreens: The best, most convenient drugstores, with high profit per customer visit.

- Wells Fargo: Running a bank like a business, with a focus on the western USA.

- Abbott Laboratories: To excel at creating products that contribute to cost-effective health care.

- Joy Farming: To inspire and equip leaders to lead with joy in the worlds they impact.

After we share our statements, we have an open discussion. People normally are very introspective at this stage. Their minds are still churning. They seem to be still digesting. We remark on that. I again mention that this is a journey—a journey that can take time to complete. It is, however, very necessary to work with the statement developed.

This will start your journey. It is powerful already and can be refined as you move forward.

And, I learnt all of this as a little boy. I just didn't realize the powerful lesson I was being taught. Every person on the farm had a specific purpose on the farm when the sheep had to be sheared. The passion was there. People were within their own gifts and talents.

Everyone was working in their *sweet spot* to ensure that this intricate dance of animals and humans could be concluded in good time and with great results.

When we can emulate this in life and in business, it does not feel like work. We are engaged. We are energized. Soon the joy starts flowing ...

Your Own Joy Plan – Ensure Joy in Your Life

Your Short-Term Joy Plan – Starting New Joy Habits: I am huge proponent of what is called the 90-day plan. We use this handy tool all the time with our MacKay CEO Forums members. I use it for my own development and coach my clients to do the same. It makes sense to me that our brains find it easy to remember three things—we can wrap our minds relatively easily around three concepts. It has also been proven that if you cannot change your behaviour in 90 days, your chances of ever changing that behaviour are very slim indeed.

Table 1 90-day Plan Format

Goal	How will you measure success?	Who will be able to help you achieve success?	Your next step
Professional			
1.			
2.			
3.			
Family			
1.	a		
2.			
3.			
Personal			
1.			
2.			
3.			

What I want to encourage you to do is take what you've read up to now, and choose which of these concepts (I call them "joy seeds") resonate with you, list them, and choose some to apply in your life over the next 90 days. Do you need to do some work to get more grit? Do you want to master your emotions? Is lack of time mastery holding you back? Do you want to improve your relationships? Perhaps you need to develop your own purpose and/or *sweet spot* statements?

Choose a least one goal for each of the three areas of your life: professional, family, and personal. Start small, but be as specific as possible. I always use the SMART[18] acronym to test that my goals are up to standard.

Then describe what success will look like when you achieve it. This picture will be essential to inspire you to work towards the goal; it can motivate you when the going gets tough and the distractions start clamouring for your attention.

Next, determine who will be able to help you achieve that success. I advise picking a person who will not only be able to encourage you, but also knows you well, loves you, acknowledges your quirks, and will hold you accountable. Tough love is needed here to ensure growth! Look for people who are willing to become your partners in your pursuit of joy. Naturally for professional goals, these partners will be found amongst your associates, colleagues, and peers. For family goals, spouses or significant others,

[18] S-Specific, M-Measurable, A-Achievable or Attainable, R-Relevant or Realistic, T-Time-bound

siblings, cousins, or other family members should feel honoured if you ask them. For personal goals, those closest to you will be in the best position to help you and hold you accountable. It may be the person you live with or the person you see very regularly.

Lastly, identify your next step and share it with the person you've chosen. This first step, and the movement towards it, is crucially important.

Your joy-finding journey has started!

Over the next 90 days, work through your plan. Place a reminder in your calendar, to revisit at least once per month, to give feedback to your joy partners. Keep at it, celebrate every success along the way, and soon you will start feeling happier and more fulfilled. Before you know it, the first seeds will sprout, and your daily life will become more joyous!

Once your first 90-day plan has been completed, revisit, regroup, and repeat the process. Build your next plan using the same format. Focus now on seeing which of your goals have put you on the path of establishing new joy-bringing habits. Cement those in your life.

This is now also the time to shift your focus outward, away from your own needs. Look for opportunities to spread what you are learning to those you work with, your family members, and those closest to you. Look for opportunities to bless those who were willing to be your joy partners. Look for opportunities to bless those who will never be able to bless you back. Plant joy seeds all over your world. Some will sprout. Some will not. Worry not, keep planting. Arrive at each appointment ready to spread joy. Enter every room, virtual or physical, on the lookout for opportunities to plant those seeds of joy.

Soon your life will be so much happier. Your focus will shift from your own needs to recognizing those around you. You will become the person who sees a colleague or staff member showing up without their regular spark. You will become the person who encourages and supports. Your own joy will start growing outwards.

I have found that by focusing on helping others find joy, my own journey has become so much better. Worries, doubts—all those negative joy stealers—have not received any oxygen. Instead my joy has grown through all the joy seeds I learnt to plant wherever I go. Some of those planted for me. Most planted to spread joy all around.

Your Long-Term Joy Plan – Living With Joy: Almost all businesses I work with have Strategic Plans with specifics for the next year and goals for the next three to five—even as far out as ten—years. It's considered a requirement for success.

Business plans are used routinely.

When we move into the personal sphere, many people will have financial plans to make sure they have enough financial resources for retirement.

Yet, I do not know of many people who have a Strategic Plan for themselves or for their families. We seem to be good at planning for business or financial success, but when it comes to taking best care of those aspects right under our noses, we seem to falter.

Do you know your personal strengths and weaknesses? Do you periodically list your opportunities and threats? Do you strategize how you can use your strengths to face your threats and to make best use of your opportunities? What issues are you facing? How can you solve those?

Have you ever done this for you or for your family?

My challenge to you would be to use what you have learnt throughout the 90-day plan, sit down, and plan where you want to be at the end of your life on this planet, by answering questions like:

- Where do you want to be?
- What do you want to do with the rest of your life to have a maximum impact?
- What legacy do you want to leave behind?

A useful exercise here, albeit a bit dark perhaps, is to pretend you are writing the eulogy for your own funeral or celebration of life. What do you want the content of that to be? Where do you need to course correct now to be able to get there?

Put what you learn into your long-term plan. Remember to use SMART goals and include the people who will help you get there. Discuss it with them, and you will be on your way!

Your joy will start growing as you come closer to what you want to be like at the end of your life. You will start spreading it to the people you want to have a positive impact on and those who will help you get there!

Eternal Joy: When I was a Rotarian[19] we were advised that three subjects should be avoided at all cost, as they bring a serious risk of division in your club. The topics of sex, politics, and religion were known as the three taboos. These topics have proven over many years to focus on people's differences, instead of binding them together. Rotary was founded to help businesspeople work better together, and I have found that these three taboos pretty much apply to modern business as well. You are not supposed to talk about them!

If you, however, want to achieve eternal joy, we need to at least discuss one, or rather the cousin of one of those taboos. What you believe in the eternal sense is vitally important here? Some of us call it our faith. It is closely related to religion. I, however, do not want to discuss religion, especially not religious differences, as it is a major divider between people on this planet! Instead I want to focus on what you believe in the eternal sense. I am intentionally keeping this part super simple and at the surface, as I'd rather find what binds us together than go into anything that divides us as a species. All I want to explore is our beliefs and how it will serve us to find more joy.

What do you believe? Here are some options:

1. You believe there is a God. What you call Him (or him) or Her (or her) and how you worship is not important for our purposes here.

2. You believe there is no god or God.

---

[19] https://www.rotary.org/en

3. You believe in eternal life. How this will work is again not important for our purposes here.

4. You believe there is no such thing as an afterlife.

With this as a perspective, it is time to develop a plan to prepare yourself to be ready for whatever you believe in.

With this approach, if you, for example, believe that there is no afterlife, it becomes so much more important that you have as many experiences as possible during your life on earth to bring yourself and your loved ones joy. A bucket list becomes so much more important, as opposed to if you believe you will have unbelievable experiences after your death. If you believe in an afterlife, somehow a bucket list becomes less important, as your energy will perhaps be spent on activities to prepare you for your afterlife.

I personally am preparing to meet my Maker in person after my death. My plan, therefore, includes an eternal relationship component. I am studying the Bible. I am in a relationship with my Creator through prayer; this is what I choose to do. I am excited to be able to prepare in this way. It brings me joy. It allows me to spread joy to people and situations when odds may be stacked against me. It doesn't matter. My eternal perspective gives me that big-picture vision. I am preparing for something much bigger and much more magnificent than the ordinary. Here, on earth, I get immense joy from worshipping God and cannot wait to be together again after COVID-19 with my friends, praising God with our music through our choir and orchestra.

This is my outlook. My choice. What is yours?

Think how you can use your choice to equip yourself to show up with joy and be able to spread it wherever you go.

The Joys of the Worship Choir

It was during one of our songs that it struck me: I am part of one amazing team effort, and it feels great!

I was just one tenor voice in an eighty-member choir, supported by a sixty-eight-member orchestra, and an eight-person band, ten lead singers, and for a few songs, our nearly 100 youth singers; a tiny cog in a giant wheel. We were all hanging on the lips, the gestures, every nuance, and expression on his face. The whole being of our fearless leader, conductor, encourager, and disciplinarian: our worship pastor was in his element again!

The concentration was complete. One wrong note, one too-early entry, could spoil the joyful music we were producing. Our contribution, to help prepare people's hearts for the message, was an important part of the service.

Our leader keeps us together with discipline, skill, tons of humour, and humility. His joy is infectious, and one wants to do one's best for him. He pushes us out of our comfort zones and is there to encourage us when we falter.

Do check us out on www.willingdon.org under media. It is guaranteed to bring some joy into your life as well!

Your Next Steps to Keep Finding Joy

Look for opportunities to spread what you are learning to those you work with, your family members, and those closest to you. Look for opportunities to bless those who were willing to be your joy partners. Look for opportunities to bless those who will never be able to bless you back. Plant joy seeds all over your world. Some will sprout. Some will not. Worry not, keep planting. Arrive at each appointment ready to spread joy. Enter every room, virtual or physical, on the lookout for opportunities to plant those seeds of joy.

Soon the harvest will become noticeable. Very soon it will become bountiful. It will come full circle when it starts providing the seeds for next year's crops.

This book was written to not only tell you more about how to farm with joy (like my *Oupa* did), but most importantly, how to use these tools to make your life as a leader, and the lives of those you lead and love, richer, more fulfilling, and above all things, more joyful.

Now go off and go plant those seeds that will sprout joy for you and yours. But, before you start, remember you first have to prepare the soil!

Acknowledgements

Just as a village is needed to bring up a child, a whole crowd was needed to get this book to the finish line!

This book would not have happened without the unstinting love and support of my wife, Estelle. And the encouragement of my mom, Sarie, and the rest of the family, especially my brother, Johann, and my kids, Jurie and Lili. Thank you also to my godmother and aunt, Annette Oudkerk, for sharing her memories of the farm.

Nancy MacKay must be mentioned next. She has been amazing in her support, mentorship, encouragement, and by constantly challenging me over a period of nearly twenty years. Thank you for selflessly sharing and for showing the way.

Then there are my board members! Thank you, Scott Brown, for always trusting me and believing in me. Thank you, Shelley McDade, for your nonplussed way of getting me to just get on with it and get it done. Thank you, Simon Dannatt, for quietly opening doors and opportunities. Thank you, Lesley Nolan, for your constant enthusiasm and bringing of resources. Thank you, Luke O'Hare, for thoughtfully considering every latest ploy this Human has come up with again and for diplomatically making your point a consideration. The five of you are changing my career and my life for the better. All I can say is thank you.

Thank you, Natalie Meixner, for being my first client and for coming back for more. You are a phenomenal and a brave leader, and I learn a ton from you. Thank you, Jim Bindon, for planting the image of the sailboat in the GritGraphic© during one of our sessions together!

Thank you to all my MacKay Forum members and other clients who constantly inspire me with how you make this planet of ours a better place every day.

Thank you to my team members Johann Human, Eske Cilliers, Tamara Stephen and Kim Fontaine. You are all helping me be better, day by day. Thank you for caring and accepting me for who I am.

Thank you to my colleagues across the continent. There are too many to mention, but I do want to list my posse mates: Steve Foran, Tim Kist, Kerry Brown, Bernie Kollman, Katie Bennett, Tim Dumas, Colin Cox, Oliver Baezner, and Ross Montagano. You guys inspire me every day!

Thank you to Pastors Norm Schmidt (for reading the manuscript) and Ray Harms-Wiebe, with the Willingdon, team for your encouragement, wisdom, and leadership. Thank you also to dear friends Colin and Cathy Alexander for always encouraging and discussing concepts.

And lastly thank you to all you readers and watchers of my little videos. I am grateful to be on this journey of life with you!